EXPAT LARRY

To Charlotte,
   May all your future
travels be amazing.

               Larry   Sept '15

LAWRENCE TURNER

ISBN: 1500998915
ISBN 13: 9781500998912

To my mum (mom), Olive June Turner, born 24th June 1928, who makes a great cup of tea. Thanks for your memories.

TABLE OF CONTENTS

PREFACE

ON TWEETING

> "I tweet, therefore my entire life has shrunk to 140 character
> chunks of instant event & predigested gnomic wisdom. & swearing."
> @NeilGaiman

I am a Twit. Have been for several months as I write this, exiled in London, Ontario, Canada. For the past five months. Only one to go. I miss my little English home. Some would say I've always been a twit, but here I refer to the art of Tweeting on Twitter. Like so many of my generation, I swore never to Tweet. Facebook was bad enough. Still don't know how to use it effectively. Same goes for Twitter. Don't get it. Not all of it anyway. But slowly, little by little, it becomes clearer. Astounding that someone types something and someone else responds, or at least reads what that person Tweets. I started with no followers and now have 170 hanging off every word I type (since writing that last year, I now have 650).

Well, that isn't quite true. I thought I'd give Twitter a go, get the word out about my first book and then shut it down. What I didn't know at first was how succinct Twits had to be. The Twitter powers-that-be give us 140 characters, which include letters, punctuation and spaces to spill our guts, plead our case, get our point across, impress the hoi polloi and generally make sense. My last sentence would have made it to the end of the word 'our' before the word 'point'.

I learned quickly to be pithy. Cleverness came with practice. But not every time. Took me a year to learn about hashtags and how to work people in with @. Still confusing. I've had Irish guys cyber bully me, authors message me and celebrities ignore me. But I don't give up. I don't go on as much as I did in the beginning. That's true of any new thing….lots of activity until the novelty wears off. It has, though, taught me to be more concise.

And that's why this book of helpful, culturally inspired notes and short essays is to the point. Mostly. Pithy sentences. Rotten grammar. Misplaced participles, in the wrong tense. Preposition ending phrases. Stephen Fry might approve. Not sure. Expat Larry, the Twit, shall endeavour to entertain, enlighten, enthrall and end any misconceptions anyone has regarding cultural differences between his two homelands. Much of it anyway. All this in the new prose. The pithy, succinct, never redundant, running prose. Enjoy (as it is stated in North American Speak). A third country has been thrown into the mix, France, where Expat Larry lived for 5 years in the 1980s. BTW (By the way in Twittalk), the two homelands are England (not Great Britain or the UK) and Canada. Larry has a stake in both.

The very name Larry evokes guffaws on both sides of the ocean. The English have an expression, 'Happy as Larry'. The first written record of the phrase was from New Zealand, but might have come from Australia, then on to Britain. Something about an Australian pugilist named Larry who never lost a fight. He was happy. Really doesn't matter how it began because now the sentiment is everywhere and fixed. Another phrase is 'Last minute Larry', not flattering at all. A woman used it the other day in a casual conversation at the local train station. What does she know?

Even in North America the Larrys portrayed on television or in the movies are usually as hapless as they may be happy because of it. When Larry appears on the screen we laugh. Most of the Larrys on Facebook are of African American descent. Seems when the white American parents gave up on the name Larry for their kids, the black American parents took it over. You understand, of course, that Lawrence and Larry are the same thing. Friends of Lawrence Olivier called him Larry. Our Larry's friends call him Larry. In High School he cringed at the beginning of the year as they called out the names to assign each to his/her Form. Back then Larry was acceptable. Lawrence was like Clarence….dumb.

The years they called out Lawrence, Larry thought he would die. He didn't. Now it's his name of choice. More regal, substantial, esoteric. Except that people now think it pompous and pretentious. He can't win.

Hopefully, Larry will emerge from these pages as someone to be envied, pitied, emulated, frowned upon, championed, sought after, laughed at, laughed with, scorned, knighted, forgiven, loved and above all entertaining. But never ignored. His take on life in both parts of the world in which he has lived has its place in the echelons of anthropological studies, even though his observations are anything but scholarly and his musings are never above reproach or scorn.

You may have noticed a switch from speaking about myself in the first person to the third person. That's because there are moments of candid personal data revealed of which I want no part. A detached look at things is better than becoming directly involved. Besides, there are parts of Larry's life and his ways that even I laugh at and ridicule. He is such a character let me tell you. If anyone lives up to the name Larry, he does. Why do you think I am once again Lawrence? Well, there you are then.

I have relied almost entirely on Larry's memory of things. Where things grew fuzzy, his mum was consulted. Her memory of the past is sharper at 86 years than Larry's at 63. But then, as she says, she has had more time lately to sit and think about the past and to process it, especially since Larry's dad died nearly four years ago. She was his partner for 67 years, married for 63 of those and was in love with his dad since she was 12. Bless her. Larry, on the other hand, has led a much more colourful life. I have tried not to embellish any of the stories herein. And I apologise for any indiscretions revealed that may offend. Larry sends his regrets too. So does Randy, but more of him later.

And that, my friends, is the essence of the tales and information about to unfold. Hang on, it's quite a ride. Where it ends depends on you.

140 characters exactly in that last paragraph. This Twit is learning.

CHAPTER 1

Roots And Beginnings

"Afoot and lighthearted I take to the open road, healthy, free, the world before me." Walt Whitman

The old Empire (or at least the Commonwealth) is not quite dead yet. Not even Scotland can escape the fold. Britain is on the move again. Look out world. Just when you think the old girl is about to give up the ghost, she turns the page to begin a new chapter, keeping the world interested in her exploits. Why the female moniker? Larry likes to think of this island as a woman. Such a tiny island too. The whole of the United Kingdom can fit into his Province of Ontario, Canada, just over four times and is considered one of the leading nations on the planet, even if it is a self-professed declaration. Rule Britannia, if it can only maintain the momentum.

The proof is in the pudding as they say. A more than successful Diamond Jubilee for Queen Elizabeth II and the world coming to play games in London during the summer of 2012 are more than enough proof that Britain still has what it takes to capture the attention and imagination of the entire planet. Let's not forget Harry Potter, The Beatles, the incessant Rolling Stones, the ubiquitous David Beckham and all the Brits who keep winning Oscars year after year, Daniel Day Lewis the latest to be feted in that capacity, while not forgetting

Dame Judy Dench and Dame Helen Mirren plus all the James Bonds. We shall not mention the Falkland Islands (still British at the time of writing).

Larry lives in the midst of all the excitement in a rather forgotten part of London….the Borough of Bexley in the southeast of England and London. Overlooked by politicians and celebrities, it has certainly not been ignored according to its history. The Borough of Bexley and indeed all of southeast London remains an important ingredient in the great British experience. Few write books, movie or TV scripts about the Borough of Bexley, but that is about to change. This is the story of Expat Larry and his take on life in his corner of this southeast section of London, this small part of the County of Kent, its people and their role in the Great British Tapestry. Larry also helps us examine its place in the wider context of cultural settings, comparing it to other English speaking cultures and one French culture. First, though, where does Larry come from and how did he get back there?

Larry was born on this island of the Brits near Hampton Court in the south-west part of London, England. Unremarkably. Not royalty for sure. His parents lived in East Sheen, a little town in Surrey, just down the road from Hampton Court. He went back there on his sixtieth birthday. Not much had changed. The little white cottage, with its playhouse at the bottom of the garden, across the road from his old home on Coulson Road was gone. In its place stood a row of townhouses. Everything changes. But the neighbourhood looked essentially the same. Faces have evolved. Different ethnic groups replaced the sea of white from the 1950s. Shop names had changed, probably many times. The old drain and sewage pipes on his balcony were still there and the steps leading up to the house remained the same. For a moment, time froze.

Meanwhile, little Larry, at three years of age in 1954, wandered East Sheen's High Street (Upper Richmond Road). His mother to this day agonises over her lack of attentiveness. But these were more innocent times in the mid nineteen fifties. In most places anyway. They must have been in this part of London. Larry walked, by himself, out the door, down the steps onto Coulson Road, turned left along to Penrhyn Crescent and left again to Upper Richmond Road. He would sit on the corner, watched over by a flower seller, checking the socks of male passersby. He had once seen a man with different coloured socks walk by and the fascination continued. When a man stopped to buy flowers, Larry would lift his trouser legs to check for odd socks. Oh the psychological implications.

Not a career that has any future. Neither was releasing the neighbours' Guinea Pigs. Early animal rights protestation? What Larry had going for him was smarts. Big smarts for a little guy. He memorised a book of poetry at age three. OK, so it was The Green Umbrella, but it was a start. Might have been a Mozart. His mum played piano and sang in a small Production Company known as The Merrymakers. Music came later for Larry. So, no Mozart then. Meanwhile, he enjoyed his own company, watching lorries (trucks) rumble up and down the High Street outside their window. When he was 2 ½ years old, his little brother was born. He got the good name. With Larry's mum looking after his brother and his dad away at work, he was left to his own devices.

The extended family lived in the southeast of London around Deptford. Larry's mum and dad decided to act all posh and move west, even joining a tennis club out that way. The rest of the family thought them toffee-nosed, a derisive term for English people who consider themselves above the rest. Larry's dad called his mum's side of the family 'the herd'. Relatives visiting from the east were told to keep silent or speak in low tones. Larry was particularly obnoxious, instructing aunts, uncles and cousins in proper elocution. Needless to say, Larry's nuclear family didn't have many visitors. One aunt stayed over quite often to look after Larry. At the age of three, he loved to confound her with words no three-year-old should know. "Say preposterous, auntie," he'd say. "Now spell it."

Larry proceeded to torture his aunt by correcting her pronunciation. He was branded as precocious. Too intelligent for his age. Might have been a future Prime Minister of all the Britons. Could possibly have been the next great English thinker or philosopher. Things could not have been better for him until one day a stranger came to town. A fast talking, smooth operating Canadian with American pretensions.

Larry's dad was a shoe man. He sold shoes for the Bata shoe company in Richmond, Surrey, down the road from East Sheen. Bata shoes had begun in the now defunct Austro-Hungarian Empire, later Czechoslovakia, moving the headquarters to Canada after the Second World War. Being an artist, Larry's dad had a flare for decorating. He won awards for his window dressings. It attracted the

3

attention of shoe giants from all over Britain and apparently from the colonies too. The world might have been his dad's oyster.

The Canadian acted as if he were a representative of the Bata shoe company, but was actually a rogue shop owner and a poacher. He offered Larry's dad the Moon and some of Venus if he would come to Canada and manage his chain of shops. Turns out he only had one, in a little plaza in Willowdale, Ontario. All promise and little substance. Big talkers do that. They rarely deliver. Larry gives his dad credit for staying with it for a while. He would work in one other shoe store before eventually finding his place in his God's shop, the church. Larry's dad became a preacher. That never would have happened if they'd stayed in England.

Larry's dad grabbed at the chance to live overseas and in 1955, just after Larry's fourth birthday in March, his dad headed off on the Queen Mary for New York then on to Toronto, Canada. The rest of the family followed in July aboard the SS Scythia, sailing its last voyage, landing in Montreal, taking the train from there to Toronto. Larry's posh accent wasn't appreciated in the New World. When his dad greeted them at Union Station in Toronto, he told Larry not to talk so loud. The shoe was on the other foot. He meant Larry should lose his accent. He says he could hear his aunt chuckling to herself. For some reason, there was a Limey back-lash in Canada in the mid-1950s. Larry soon learned to speak the local lingo with a Canadian accent. But he never really felt Canadian until 1967, Canada's Centennial, when the whole family became Canadian citizens. Larry was 16.

Little Larry was essentially raised in the church in Canada even before his dad became a preacher, but that's for another chapter. Suffice it to say Larry's early life was skewed by visions of otherworldliness rather than the world about him. Given his shy and rather introverted nature, much like his dad's, he relished the sheltered existence of church life. It protected him from the nasty world outside. Not that he didn't take the occasional peek around out there, envying the naughtiness if not the nastiness.

Larry's memories of the homeland faded as he tried to fit into the New World culture. The language was different there. Sure they spoke English, but it had a funny sound to it, like people spoke with marbles in their mouths and actually said 'marble' a lot. No good correcting everybody. He'd just have to fit in. Not an easy task for an immigrant kid in a land that seemed to spread out forever. So big that crossing a street seemed like traversing the ocean. Some people wanted to hear him talk in that English accent. They thought it was cute. They were usually girls and grownups. The boys just thought it was odd and unacceptable. Larry always ran away from fights that would defend his honour. Kids can be cruel.

Larry hid in his world of British made Dinky Toys and a newfound love, television. He could be anybody while watching TV. Rin Tin Tin gave him a love of dogs. Superman, starring George Reeves and Mighty Mouse taught him bravery. The Howdy Doody Show and Kukla, Fran and Ollie presented Larry to North American humour. The Micky Mouse Club introduced him to the world of entertaining and friendships like that of Spin and Marty. Leave it to Beaver offered a sense of morality. Larry watched The Ed Sullivan Show with his family. He wanted so badly to be on stage and become famous. The Roy Rogers Show confused him. He wondered how cowboys on horses and Pat Brady's Nellybelle the jeep could exist in the same era. He did enjoy the program Fury, about a horse and a boy. More morality. Not always a bad thing as long as it's not lop-sided in favour of someone's particular brand of morality.

Seems the whole point of kids TV in the late fifties was to moralise. Conspiracy? Who knows? It all had to be wholesome. The censors back then were merciless. Larry didn't seem to mind too much. It became a theme of his as he grew up. A happy world full of happy people who solve small problems effortlessly, where everyone listens to and acts on sage advice, where the good guys always win, where death never ends the journey. He's sort of glad he finally grew up to face some semblance of reality. But he says 'not too much, thank you very much'. Besides, reality can be so limiting.

Outer Space took over Larry's life in the sixties. On television anyway. A fascination that remains with him to this day. Because he was so useless with Maths and Sciences in High School, he gave up on the idea of becoming an Astronomer or an Astrophysicist. The idea of being whizzed around in one of those gyro gizmos deterred him from applying to be an astronaut. That and he wasn't an American with aviation experience. He turned to the other great show of the sixties…..music. That's when he fell in love with his homeland all over again.

The first band he played in did three Beatles tunes. That's the night one of the great looking girls in Larry's High School approached him for an autograph and a kiss….a great kiss he emphasises. He was hooked. The Mersey Beat was his new passion, followed by the likes of Led Zeppelin, Joe Cocker, Jethro Tull, The Rolling Stones, Eric Clapton and Ten Years After to name only a few. He envied his cousins in England having access to Carnaby Street, The Marquee Club, The Scotch of St. James and all the small venues that hosted Blues and Rock bands in those swinging 60s days. He swore to himself that one day he would go back there to live.

It wasn't until 1973 that Larry returned to England. He was 22 years old. None of his cousins followed music like he did. They were pub crawlers. Being raised in a rather strict Christian home, Larry had never taken a drink. But his English cousins changed all that. Back then Newcastle Brown Ale (founded by Colonel Porter who died the same year Larry went back to England) was much higher in alcohol content. One of his cousins took him to a pub in Soho and plied the lad with not one but three of the strong ales. His first inebriating experience. He says he liked it. A lot.

The rest of that trip was about one pub after another, even on the way to and from one of Larry's cousin's wedding in Birmingham. At the wedding reception back in London, one of Larry's uncles kept him supplied with suds all night. He would hand Larry a pint and say, "Don't worry son. I'll tell your mum and dad you drank lemonade all night." Good old soul he was. He died that same year in November. Larry mourned back in Canada. He was missing his English family. He had grown up in Canada for 17 years without grandparents, aunts, uncles and cousins around unlike the other kids he knew in Canada.

That first trip cemented Larry's love for his homeland. He didn't mind that everything was so much tinier than in Canada. Deptford Park was not the spacious place he remembered as a four-year-old. The houses were crammed together, the streets so very narrow. London smelled of Diesel and smoke every day. You couldn't get a decent hamburger and Britain was still miles behind North America technologically speaking. It mattered not to Larry though. He loved the quaintness, the history of the place, rediscovered family and how close everything was to the sea. And, oh yes, the pubs….so many pubs. Oldey Worldy pubs and the local up the road from his Nan's place, the Rose of Kent. It's gone now, turned into flats (apartments). Not the same. Everything changes.

Speaking of Larry's Nan (grandmother), the one on his mum's (mom's) side. She once asked Larry about life in Canada. Never one lost for words, she began chatting to Larry the moment he arrived at her door in Deptford after a long flight from Canada. He stayed with her for the entire month during his time in England except for side trips. She spilled her life history in those first hours and every bit of family gossip along with it. All this while she fussed over pots of tea and cakes, the likes of which Larry had never tasted. You can keep your hamburgers, he thought. All the females on his Nan's side are chatterboxes. She wanted to know if Canadians in the Colonies still lived in log cabins and got about in stage coaches.

That was in 1973. Larry said he supposed some Canadians lived in log cabins and then only by choice. Maybe not riding in stage coaches though. Not where he lived in Canada anyway. But young people in North America were still trying to get back to nature and the land in those heady days following the sixties. Lots of land and space still available. Not so on the island of Larry's birth. Immigration was picking up post Second World War. Less space in which to fit an ever growing population. He noticed none of this back then. He was too busy staring at pretty English ladies wearing mini skirts and sampling English brew.

Larry returned to the motherland several times after that first visit. During the second visit in 1978, he went back to the house in East Sheen. The white cottage was still there. The steps up to the balcony remained along with the drain and sewage pipes. All of the few memories he had from such an early age came back. The next time he would see the place was on his 60th birthday with the changes he mentioned earlier. Nostalgia has limits. That will probably be his last visit there. Everything changes.

He only revisited the southeast of London because he had an aunt and uncle living there, in Welling where Larry presently lives, actually on the border of Bexleyheath and Welling in the Ward of St. Michaels. The forgotten Borough of Bexley. Heard of it? Not surprised you hadn't. It's just beside the Borough of Greenwich (pronounced Grenich). You've heard of that I'm sure. Greenwich mean time? The Meridian? More of Bexley later. Larry knew nothing of it, even when visiting his aunt and uncle (the same aunt whose diction he used to correct). He just knew Welling. No one has heard of Welling either. Before the 19th century there was nothing much there, just forest mostly. Not until after the First

World War did any human growth occur. Larry's house was built in the 1930s by a man who went to prison for using inferior building materials. Nothing changes.

New beginnings in the southeast. It isn't the southwest, but it's home to Larry. He wasn't sure what he was going to do when he arrived 8 years ago. He came for a new start. Not much was familiar. He would need to find work. That was before the great Credit Crunch that hit the global economy around 2007-2008. He found that work in 2006 in an unlikely setting, but the best he could have imagined for the time. A music shop in what was back then the largest mall in Europe, Bluewater. Selling guitars, other music gear and teaching guitar lessons. Larry learned one very valuable lesson while working in the shop. Retail is not for him. On his feet for hours, customer abuse, low pay (cheap boss) and silly hours. But with all that, he is grateful for the first job of his new beginnings.

Most customers guessed Larry's accent as Irish. He says he's never figured that one out. He learned a lot about the music business from the savvy blokes working with him. The blokettes working there were for show. That was the cheap guv'nor's (boss's) idea. He even said as much. "You lads are the brains", he told the blokes, "but the totty will bring them in." The guv was a piece of work to be sure. He knew very little about music, being an entrepreneur first. He told his staff that he might open an ice cream stand in the shop to bring in more revenue. The staff cringed.

Larry grew steadily tired of standing on his feet all day, working holidays and being paid minimum wage. Two years after his new beginnings, Larry decided to begin again. One fine day he looked at his colleagues and said, "I'm out-of-here mates. Catch you on the flip side." And he walked out in the middle of his shift. Larry took all his guitar students with him, earning more in a day than he had all week in the shop. The music shop didn't last much longer. The guv, it seems, spent too much of the profits on his personal lifestyle. He couldn't keep the shop, his Mercedes and his high rental flat (apartment) in a swank neighbourhood expecting to remain solvent. Larry now had his own business, adding a studio at the back of the garden. His own little white cottage and playhouse. Larry was home.

Growing up in Canada had its advantages. Canadians, by and large, have a very neutral view on many of the issues the world sees as important enough to war over. Many Canadians don't see the big whoop when it comes to that. Canadians take 'live and let live' very seriously. They also have diversity in cultural experiences much like the Swiss, but over vaster territory and less homogeneous, although the Swiss might argue that German, French and Italian cultures are as diverse as you could possibly imagine. How Canadians have managed to maintain one nation, keeping it together, says more about laissez-faire than it does about anything concerning national unity.

Some, but never enough, French Canadians want a separate state. Most French Canadians know they wouldn't last five minutes on their own and continue to vote down separation every time it hits the political stage. The usual cry for independence comes mainly from the rebellious youth who blame Canadian federalism for a lack of jobs or university students who think they know better than the more sensible, average French Canadian who understands from where his or her income and benefits come.

First Nations Canadians continue to be an enigma during the early stages of the twenty-first century. Except for trying to reclaim lands that were taken from them, the various bands can never decide amongst themselves what they really want and can never agree what they would do with land returned to them. Larry imagines they would just become the next bunch of greedy developers like the bunch we have already. Most First Nations people simply want respect and a place to live in peace. The greedy ones from every cultural background want cash. When it comes to it, what we see happening in this widely spread, diversely cultural experience, or mosaic as Canadians understand it, is a tolerance that accepts separatists and reclaimers, hockey lovers and hockey haters, carnivores and vegans, gays and straights and people of faith and atheists under one ugly flag, singing 'O Canada', drinking beer and placing fourth in everything on the world stage.

Some of those things might apply to the United Kingdom, an oxymoron if ever one existed. Though generally not as laid-back as the average Canadian, Brits exist in a forced harmony that may never again see the unity displayed at the 2012 summer Olympic games in London. The island is as diverse culturally and regionally different as any nation on earth. Politically, the United Kingdom comprises four small countries, England, Scotland, Wales and Northern Ireland. Regionally, England is broken into The North, The Midlands, The South and Cornwall (The West). These tentative and arbitrary boundaries can be disputed and subdivided by anyone with an opinion on such matters, but Larry thinks the four areas of England suffice to make his point.

Scottish, Welsh and Irish regionalism definitely exists. The Isle of Skye in Scotland, for example, is a tiny world of its own, but my primary concern is with the land of my birth, England. That's not to say many Scots, Welsh and even Cornish peoples want to stay British. Cornwall is a part of England, but wishes it weren't. Independence parties are ever present especially in Scotland and Wales, both countries having their own Legislatures and Scotland its own Parliament. Northern Ireland is an enigma, part of the United Kingdom, but distinctly Irish. Larry grew up with the fiery Ian Paisley making trips to Canada to stir up Protestant hatred toward Roman Catholics in Ireland and raising money to fight them. Larry was never sure about his true agenda. He just remembers an angry man speaking with a guttural Irish lilt pleading with Irish Protestants and the rest to join the cause. He was a Presbyterian as was Larry's family by this time and they were ashamed of his rhetoric. Canadian Irish Presbyterians were more sympathetic owing to their past experiences in the old country. People don't seem to be able to let go of the past. It will be humanity's undoing.

Northern Ireland goes from one crisis to the next. As this is being written, there is more unrest. It's not worth going into the reasons why. History repeats. It seems doomed to do so and not only because of religious differences. Whole families in parts of England continue to vote as their fathers and fathers' fathers voted even if their political party spouts rubbish (read 'talks garbage' for North Americans). It may be that all politicians lie, knowingly or otherwise, deliberately deceiving the ignorant masses into believing their rather vague and often unrealistic promises. It could be they truly believe in what politicians say and are themselves hopelessly and helplessly naïve. No matter the rhetoric, the outcome is always the same….the economy is good then times are good or at least tranquil, the economy goes bad and crime goes up and the hoi poloi become restless. History repeats and no politician has the will to change the status quo. If they start out with the ambition to overhaul the political system in either the British or Canadian Parliaments, the juggernaut that is the landed gentry or corporate oligarchs soon puts all potential world changers in their place.

The title of this book could easily have been Triple Expat Larry because he lived in France for five years in the 1980s. Five years is long enough to get the feel for a place, especially if the language of that particular culture is learned. Though we are now in a new millennium, French attitudes and tendencies remain the same, ingrained feelings of superiority and entitlement, under laid with an inferiority complex that would shatter the state if acknowledged. Remember, this is a country that has lost almost every war it has ever fought. The French, though, recall battles won, never wars lost. They do like to remind Larry about William the Conqueror's victory over King Harold on English turf at Battle near Hastings and his subsequent occupation of the country. He says he'll give them that one even though it has always been known as the invasion of the Normans, and Brits still speak English which grates on French nerves.

Don't misunderstand Larry. The French have so much to offer the world, including a beautiful language, more musical than English, and cheeses galore for cheese lovers. The wines are cheap and fine, the weather agreeable and even some of the people are tolerable, more notably in the south. The 1980s were a great time to live in France. The Left broke the Right's stranglehold on French political power and for a moment fresh air was breathed into the stale old Republic. Revolutionary Marianne now faced left instead of right on postage stamps and made-for-TV films showcased the lives of left-leaning artists, philosophers and celebrities instead of crusty old right-leaning personalities. Young people actually moved from the place of their birth even if it were only to the next town or city. Ridiculously, television programs examined the new phenomena. Those on the right were scandalised. Those on the left hailed it as the dawn of a new era for France. The expats giggled into our café au lait.

Regionalism is as much a part of French culture as it is in the UK and Canada. People of the south, du Midi, have little time for haughty northerners. They call northerners (Parisians) Les Parigots. The Alsace region is in a world of its own, trapped between Germany and France. Wars between the French and the Germans over the centuries have seen the territory change sides more times than the French care to admit and certainly more than the Germans dare accept.

Bretagne (Brittany) is like Cornwall in England, still very Celtic in tradition and fiercely independent. Regionalism exists to combat Federalism. It is the way of things, simplistic as these explanations may seem.

Within each nation, especially in the 21st century, different cultures band together to keep identities alive. The opening up of borders in Europe has led to an influx of migrants from poorer members of the European Union to the more wealthy (perceived as) countries. It has put such a strain on the more than generous British welfare system that the country is in danger of losing its National Health Service and has stretched the school system to breaking point. A great lack of social housing exists and much of the money earned by migrants goes back to their home countries. But all that is incidental in the face of changing social norms and an infusion of the criminal elements from European, Russian, African, Middle Eastern and Asian states that many indigenous Brits claim threaten personal and national security as well as cherished traditions. Anyway, the indigenous criminal element is more than enough for any nation to handle.

Social norms are neither good nor bad. Like most things, they develop within home-grown social milieus and are accepted as gospel until such times as the local population decides to make things otherwise. The radical changes woven into Western societies during the nineteen sixties shoved old cultural myths and morals aside to establish a new order in the form of heightened individualism and open-ended creativity, not to mention the relaxing of sexual mores like never before. When the dust of this phenomenal social revolution settled, some of the old ways were incorporated back in to the new. Some call this nostalgia, others call it not throwing the baby out with the bath water.

The best example of this in England is the guarding of the queue, a vestige of politeness held on to by Brits of all ages. Other cultures don't enshrine queuing into their table of cultural idiosyncrasies like the English. Some cultures allow pushing and shoving and queue jumping and busting to get wherever it is they need to go. They might not like someone else trying to gain the advantage by moving ahead in the queue, but their response is to push back harder. In London, where Larry lives, if someone of any culture, including British anti-social types, tries to queue jump, the muttering is politely audible and occasionally nearly belligerent. If the perpetrator is from another cultural background, the muttering may take on what some have considered racist implications, but is more usually something like, "Well, what do you expect, they don't queue where she (he) comes from." The allegation is that good manners are English and bad manners are foreign. Larry shall return to this particular piece of cultural etiquette in a later chapter.

Something Larry noticed while living in France in the 1980s was the near complete disregard for disenfranchised youth of North African descent and the restlessness of those youths in the Cités (blocks of flats or projects) of large French urban centres. It has become the price many Western nations have paid for centuries of colonialism. Ignoring the problem, like a nagging medical condition, only exacerbates the situation. When the indigenous French population voted an extreme right wing government to power again in the 1990s, the festering problem began to erupt. More than a decade into the new millennium, the seismic shock waves of this next French Revolution increase in intensity. Add to it the restlessness of the indigenous French young people and the general population who are not happy with the prevailing state of things and trouble is brewing on a massive scale. The same goes for Germany, Italy, Spain and all the major European states.

At the end of the day, week, month or year, trying to compare countries and cultures to one another is a bit like gazing at the sun and the moon and thinking they are the same thing. Even though they clearly are not, they are essentially made up of the same elements found in the whole universe. Africans, Occidentals, Orientals, indigenous and all other ethnic groups of the human race are made up of the same things as the stars. On a social level, laughter, music, story-telling and basic survival become the common factors blending all cultures into one on this tiny planet. We all may laugh at different things or have our ears tuned to different frequencies, but we share the desire to celebrate life with every culture around the world.

The problem is we don't laugh and sing enough together. We allow too many negative influences into our midst that want to agitate, disrupt and control life. The psychopaths and sociopaths of every society threaten world peace constantly. Why the majority, who want to live peacefully together, allow a few to turn the world into an armed camp is beyond me. We peace loving types do tend to give in to bullies too easily. They know it and continue to dominate. Even in so-called democratic countries, leadership has been known to bully. Despite this, people cherish freedom and individual expression. In communities where the collective rule is more important than each person's world view, everyone has idiosyncrasies that change and shape the community over time because nothing is static. The writer of the Wisdom book Ecclesiastes or Qoheleth, known as The Teacher, once said, "To everything there is a season." Bullies come and go, but love and laughter go on forever. We just have to do more of it in this age of continued cynicism and corruption.

Pessimistic view? Some would say yes, but it is the way of things. Somehow we have managed to carry on for millennia, admittedly with wasteful losses along the way. We survive because of several truths that have probably worked for humanity since the dawn of our existence on this planet. Despite politicians, dictators, oligarchs and totalitarian states, ruthless business types, unscrupulous developers, organised and disorganised crime, religions, just plain old sociopaths and psychopaths and lawyers, we who love life and see it as quirky, passion filled and even a little confusing continue to laugh, play, sing or hum, create with our minds and hands and generally enjoy ourselves to the hilt. In the words of a great song writing philosopher, "We are here for a good time, not a long time." Larry says he hears you humming the tune even now.

In the coming pages, let's explore the similarities, differences and foibles of two, for want of a better term, English cultures, the Canadian and the British arms and throw in a little French as well. Larry visited a Canadian themed pub in England a few years ago, the Maple Leaf, located on the fringes of Covent Garden in London. The tawdry décor has a charming Canadian je ne sais quoi….sports memorabilia from bygone days (Wendell Clark's hockey gear and Joe Carter's baseball cap and jersey, etc.) and a log cabin interior, even a stuffed black bear. Some hack recently painted the walls a greyish green colour ruining the effect. Still, Canadian fare is available in the form of suds and poutine. What more can you ask from a Canadian pub? The staff members seem to change every time I go in, which is less and less as the years go by. Visitors from Canada like to pay a visit.

Larry prefers The Lamb and Flag, an old English pub just up the way from The Maple Leaf but still in Covent Garden. The décor is much more authentic and very, very old world. It first became a drinking hole in 1772 under the name The

Cooper's Arms. In 1833 the name was changed to the present one. Bare Knuckled prize fights took place there early on in the 19th century, giving the pub the nickname Bucket of Blood. Larry hasn't seen a fight on the premises in all the times he's visited. Charles Dickens drank at the L&F as it's known. He got some of his material from the squalor all around the pub in his day. Now it's a chic and trendy place to shop, eat and drink.

A few years ago, Larry happened into the Maple Leaf and a very nice young lady from British Columbia was working behind the bar. Not everyone employed at the pub is an expat Canadian. But this lass was, and she had nothing good to say about Britain, England and more specifically, London.

"They're racist here, you know," she said to Larry as they became acquainted. He remarked that you find it everywhere, even in Canada. She seemed mildly put off by his statement as if he had not understood her. "I know that," she said and continued, "I mean against me, and I speak English."

"Racist against you?" Larry stammered. "How does that work?" She went on to explain how she was teased because of her accent and ridiculed for knowing little about the land in which she served (as if anyone in Essex knows more). She said she had received terrible threats from rival females who thought she dressed like a tourist and behaved like a back-woods rustic. They made wisecracks about the way she said things behind her back knowing that she heard them. They were merciless. The male species made lewd suggestions, insinuating that Canadian girls were easy (and not just on the eye). Larry pointed out to her that this was not racist, it was cultural. She was experiencing cultural differences. "They do it to each other," Larry said. "It's called banter." She was having none of it and vowed she would quit and go back to civilized British Columbia.

Not a month later Larry was back in the Maple Leaf. He asked if the young lady from BC was still working there as she was nowhere to be seen. A rather tall, lanky young man with an Australian accent said she had moved back to Canada. The news deflated Larry for a moment. Why, he thought, can't we all just get along? Then he said to himself that with such deep philosophical thoughts what he probably needed was a good bantering too.

CHAPTER 2

LONDON TO LONDON

"Sir, when a man is tired of London, he is tired of life; for there is in London all that life can afford." Samuel Johnson

"**A**re you serious?"

A friend from Toronto, Canada asked Larry this when he told him he was going to compare London, England to London, Ontario Canada.

"Well", Larry replied, "it may turn out to be a joke, but I'm serious."

"Comparing one of the biggest and most lively cities in the world to a very small city in the middle of nowhere? You're nuts. Good luck. It won't sell."

That's exactly what Larry intends to do, and especially a comparison to southeast London. Luck has nothing to do with it, nor does any remuneration. The similarities are remarkable, even if on a rather smaller scale from one to the other. It doesn't take much imagination to figure out which is the runt of the litter. People living in London, Ontario might take exception at this point, but the truth is out there.

Comparing such disparate places is more fun. Like comparing the elephant to the mouse. The strange thing is the two cities have more in common than one could imagine. Two of the commonalities aren't population and territory. The whole of London, England (known as LondonE from this point forward) comes in at nearly 8 million on 1, 538 square kilometers of land, while London, Ontario (known as LondonO from now on) has nearly ½ million people on 2,665.62 square kilometers of real-estate. You see the disparity already. Granted, much of LondonO's land is farms and small villages, but space is everything in Canada. Even the part of LondonE in which Larry now resides has a population of 1.3 million people, half that of Toronto. That is if you take in some surrounding LondonE boroughs making up the entire Southeast LondonE.

The other great difference is location. Location, location, location. What were they thinking when they planted LondonO where it is in the great scheme of things? Larry will get to that in a moment. LondonE is a hub of activity. Even though its docks along the Thames River have all gone now, except at Tilbury (where, by the way, Larry left for Canada way back in 1955), it remains accessible and close to other major centres. Not that it needs to, you understand. People come from literally everywhere to be there.

LondonO is in the middle of nowhere, surrounded, as stated earlier, by farm-land and small villages. The next closest big, important city is a 2 ½ hour drive away (Toronto), if you obey the rules of the road. Larry says that's not counting that sprawling mess they call Kitchener (was Berlin before the First World War)/ Cambridge (no university)/Hespeler/Galt/Guelph (does have a university). That area has become a city planner's nightmare and a haven for commuters who work in Toronto, another hour to the east.

LondonE is a global fashion and arts centre. LondonO is the Box Store capital of the world. Whole chunks of the city are dedicated to the Walmarts of Shoppingdom. LondonE has them too, just not as obvious. Actually, most Canadian cities are box store magnets. But LondonO is king of them all, or queen if we are to remain up-to-date. Larry guesses you have to use up all that extra space on something. So why not commerce?

Larry says he could never live in LondonO. He has seen and lived in too many other places and knows better. For all its space, he finds it too confining, like an island prison almost. Alcatraz with a few more distractions. He says that unless you have a car, you either have to hire an expensive cab, take a bus, ride a bike or walk. They may be an option for some, but Larry has issues with each. The bus, for example. In all the time he's spent in the city, he has never figured out the bus routes. 'Try and find a decipherable bus schedule and route map' he rants. They're either out-of-date, unavailable, or ridiculously convoluted, online especially. Even if the route can be deciphered, you'd be waiting ages for the next bus. Cycle lanes exist, but on the strangest selection of roads that never seem to connect. Walking is healthy, but Larry says you can spend your whole day getting places because everything is spread out and thus further away than necessary.

Larry's mum and dad moved here in July of 2000, two years after his brother and his family made the move there. Larry's brother is a Presbyterian preacher, his dad was a Presbyterian preacher. He's no longer with us. Larry is a drop-out Presbyterian preacher, giving up on God and Church during Lent of 2004. That's another story and a rather good one. Unless your vocation is still tied up in the church, the worst, thankless job ever. Then you may have trouble with Larry.

Larry's eldest daughter married a LondonO man after meeting him at a wedding there for one of her cousins, Larry's niece. She lives and works here now too, teaching people to sing properly. That means there is at least one very good reason for Larry to spend time in the middle of nowhere. His dad died in November of 2010 making it even more important that he visit his mum every so often and another good reason to visit LondonO. As I write this, Larry is there on a six month research assignment, so it is a good, long visit and allows him time to really get to know LondonO. His LondonO daughter walks to work. She can't figure out the bus routes either. Walking the 6.4 kilometre (4 mile) distance there and the same back almost every day is a haul, especially on very hot and humid days. It may be good for her health, but it does make for a very long journey. She works in a music shop. Chip off the old block. Larry is very proud of his LondonO daughter for many reasons. He hopes her band will one day visit England and turn the place upside down….musically speaking that is.

Larry has discovered one very important thing. To live in LondonO, he would have to be perpetually 21 years of age. LondonO is primarily a University town and has been since 1878. Western University (WU….you can see the connotation) used to be The University of Western Ontario (UWO and still is its legal name), but changed for reasons I don't really care to research. The problem is that foreigners, and especially those of an Oriental persuasion, think the university is out west, in the Rocky Mountains or close by. But it is in the middle of nowhere in western Ontario. He spoke to a few foreign students while roaming the campus. They all said they thought the school was in a far more exotic setting. They agreed that the campus was quite lovely, but the more exciting Toronto was too far away for a night-out-on-the-town.

Summers are OK. You can find a few nice drinking holes in the city centre, but too few for all the students at Western….nearly 30,000 of them, 12.5% of LondonO's population. That may not seem an enormous amount until you see how much the local economy depends on them each year. Many things are catered mostly to the youth at one end and a few to seniors at the other. There is no middle ground.

Larry's mum lives in a Seniors building attached to the church where his brother preaches (for another chapter). The Grocery magnates decided to close the supermarket nearby to open a cheaper version of its main stores. The area folk, especially the seniors, had to go miles for their groceries. Larry said he walked over two miles up hill both ways (really) with a back pack and a bag in each hand to get groceries. Some of the seniors took expensive cabs. Others relied on family or friends with cars. The walking might have been fine in pioneer days, but how dare the grocery magnates allow this to happen. Even when the new place opened, only half the goods previously available were offered. The prices weren't that much better either. Their own cheaper brands are rubbish.

Rant over, but you get my point. Getting around LondonO is difficult to say the least. Especially for older people. Travelling about LondonE is quite another story. But then they've had centuries to work on it and are now improving it. That's not to say it's always easy. In fact, a public transport system that works pretty well is often undermined by the automobile and overrunning engineering works on the underground (subway). Not to mention strikes and bad weather. An inch of snow in LondonE is equivalent to 50 inches in LondonO. A city built for horses and carts, LondonE has more bends in it than a pretzel. Navigating the streets in any motorized vehicle can prove tricky. All the roundabouts are confusing enough, but the narrow residential roads caused Larry to vow he'd never drive in LondonE for the rest of his life. In most places, parking is at a premium. Because Brits insist that every eligible person in each household should have a motor vehicle, many cars, vans and people carriers (just another word for van) are parked along the pavements (sidewalks).

And there are so many motor vehicles of every description on the roads. The most ridiculous for LondonE driving is the petrol/gas guzzling SUV. Larry has a red Hyundai i10. Slightly larger than those strange little Smart cars. A real senior's model. Easy to park. Good on fuel and navigates the roads rather well. But Larry doesn't drive in Britain, so it falls to his chauffeur to handle the roads like a champion rally driver. The trick is to know when to let the oncoming traffic through the narrow passageway between parked cars and when to go for it. It takes years of practice and patience. Larry has none of the latter and certainly no experience in the former. Canadian streets are much wider. I'm not going into the unwritten rules that guide this mad system of driving. Suffice it to say that if you do right, the person you let through waves a thank you or flashes his/her headlights, unless they're selfish bastards. Get it wrong and all manner of naughty finger signs and screams from open car windows greet you as you pass.

Public transport, for all its failures in LondonE, is one of the best in the world. Buses come frequently. The Underground/Tube/Subway trains arrive every few minutes and go everywhere. When there's no strike. Don't be fooled by the customised, schematic drawings of LondonE underground maps. They were produced in 1933 by Harry Beck to make sense of an otherwise pile of spaghetti lines looping all over the place and have been updated as more lines were added. Most maps of LondonE are like that. In his very large book, 'London: The Biography', Peter Ackroyd writes, '...the mapping of London represents an attempt to understand the chaos and thereby to mitigate it; it is an attempt to know the unknowable'(page 112).

Such is the plight of anyone trying to understand where anything actually is located in LondonE. LondonE underground has 11 lines, 270 stations, 249 miles (398.4 kms.) of track and runs out to Heathrow airport. Toronto has 3 lines (they say 4, but one is an over ground like the LondonE Overground and the Docklands Light Railway (DLR) which would make 13 lines for LondonE, but I'm being picky), 69 stations (including the over ground), 42.4 miles of track with plans to add another 6 stations and a short 8.6 km line by 2016. No trains to Toronto's international airport planned. That's a joke in itself.

LondonO has no subway or light rail service, something it has in common with southeast London. The forgotten Borough of Bexley (Larry's borough) has no underground and the over ground service is limited to southeastern rail, a crowded urban train. The Borough has been left out of the loop without the other services. The present Mayor just released his 35 year transport plan for LondonE. The Borough of Bexley has been left out yet again. Seven boroughs are not serviced by either the underground or the overground, six of them are south of the Thames and the borough of Bexley is the hardest hit. Larry doesn't like to whinge (whine) about these things. He can catch a bus or a train into LondonE so he's happy. Usually. Unless they're cancelled. It does happen more frequently than Larry would care to admit.

Urban trains usually run on time and are continuous, unless you live in the southeast. Larry has no complaints. Except one maybe. He wonders why they don't fumigate the cloth seats on the trains and buses after the nighttime drunks have sometimes pissed and puked on and over them. Granted, it was usually at the back of buses and the end seats of train cars, but the stench pervades. A good steam clean and some Febreze would do the job. What bothers him most is the endless cancellations he experiences from Southeastern Railways. They have by far one of the worst services of all London routes. Their personnel are generally unhelpful and can be rather rude at times. Trains break down often and sometimes drivers just don't bother showing up. Just another southeast LondonE peculiarity.

Highways (motorways) are an entirely different matter. The MacDonald Cartier Freeway, better known as Highway 401 to Ontario residents, has something like 16 lanes as it slices through Toronto and is reduced to 4 lanes at one section between Toronto and LondonO. Bottlenecking assured. They have been working for decades to make it at least 6 lanes wide, but that has been a slow process. Big transport trucks (lorries) love to take up both lanes along this section, driving fast drivers crazy. The speed limit is 100km/hr. 60mph. You can imagine the frustration when you have to drive the 100 miles plus along the route. And there are so many trucks on the highways. Big ones. Really big ones. Highway 400, no other name, going north from Toronto has six lanes at least, all the way to Barrie and slightly beyond if I recall correctly. There are plans to expand it even further.

The 401 is one of the most boring stretches of road in the world. Larry has travelled it from one end to the other, Windsor (across the river from Detroit, Michigan USA) in the west to the Quebec/Ontario border in the east. The stretch from Toronto to Windsor is the most boring and the most dangerous. Larry has nearly fallen asleep on a number of occasions driving this ribbon of highway west to Montreal and once actually did only to be awoken by his passenger. He says waking up at the wheel of a car going 75 mph is a sobering experience. And it was a tiny Toyota Corolla. And a rental.

The exit Larry takes off the 401 from Toronto into LondonO leads him to Wonderland Road. He drives the length of it to his mum's (mom's) place. Any time Larry goes back to Canada, he has to rent a car. Without a car, LondonO is a real prison. You could take a train, if you catch one at the right time, like stupid o'clock in the morning. You could fly out, but the airport is so far to the east of the city, that you may as well have driven to Toronto by the time you get to the airport, park, check your bags, wait for the flight (always delayed), get to Toronto (or wherever) wait to land, get your bags and pay an exhorbitant price to begin with for the privilege. Buses (coaches) travel a little more frequently and are relatively cheap, but again, it's getting down to the terminal and travelling to a destination in Toronto (or wherever) that leaves you leagues away from where you want to actually be. That means more public transport and so on. I use Toronto as the destination because trains don't go where you need to get and planes, well planes need airports. Buses (coaches) are the same. Never to where you need to go. So, a rental car it is.

Wonderland Road. Another oxymoron if ever one existed. There is no wonder and the land is being gobbled up by those big box stores, strip malls, donut shops, churches and apartment buildings from north to south. Traffic is always a nightmare on Wonderland and don't get Larry started on other drivers in LondonO and especially on Wonderland. It's a wonder anyone has a car left to drive the way they carry on along that stretch of road, let alone any other street, road or avenue in the city. Larry never goes near the ethnic question when speaking of bad drivers. Too clichéd and unscientific. He thinks it's the stale air from local pig farms or the fact that LondonO is such a boring city that drivers fall asleep too often to explain erratic, bad mannered driving. Cities are known to be more urban and therefore more urbane in taste and personal deployment.

One way of telling this is by the vehicles parked in the driveways (the drive). In the city, people tend to drive a more stylish model of automobile, a status symbol. Often vehicles are compact for easier parking. Vans (people carriers) are for families. The better neighbourhoods are resplendent with Mercedes, BMWs, Audis, sports cars and so on and, anyway, there is always public transportation. It is a well-known fact in Canada that the further away from the city you live, the more chance a pickup truck will be found in the driveway, maybe even a couple of pickups.

LondonE has a problem. A sort of Americanisation is taking place that has begun to have dire consequences. And I'm not just talking about American Eagle opening up in LondonE at Bluewater (you can find one in LondonO in the Masonville Mall). People are buying bigger vehicles to drive on roads that are still narrow and twisted. Small residential streets are vehicle crowded with very little parking space and hardly any drive (driveway). Large cars, SUVs, vans, people carriers and even Land Rovers and Range Rovers occupy the city, cluttering up streets, hanging over drives and across pedestrian pavements (sidewalks), polluting the air and causing accidents. All about status. Ridiculous. America's conquest of Britain. Take that Mad (Crazy) King George III (3rd).

Motorways in LondonE are a many splendoured thing. Complicated. The roundabouts as you come off them onto the 'A' roads don't help. The M25 circles the capital but seems to be more like a parking lot in places than a thoroughfare. The slip roads (on and off ramps) are dangerous. Too many lanes merging with too many drivers taking risks ensures accidents and thus delays. Motorways have numbers here as in North America and elsewhere, but have a letter before the number to designate importance and location. That's the theory anyway. 'A' roads are like spokes from the centre of LondonE going in every direction. Larry's nearest 'A' road is the A2, the London to Dover run. Main roads branching off the single number 'A' roads add a digit as their significance diminishes, up the 4 digits. The A2070 runs from a northern suburb of Ashford, Kent (the new international station for Eurorail to Paris) to the Kentish village of Brenzett. The road is only 13 miles long and began as a 'B' road until upgraded and then completely reworked in the 1990s because of the train station. It kept its 4 digits even though it ought to have only three, maybe even two digits. Such is the road system in England. Locals call the road the A Twenty Seventy. No one dares change it.

The 'M' roads are equivalent to the highways of North America, though much down-scaled. The English ones fan out from LondonE. The M1 is far less boring than the 401 to be sure, and especially the part that goes by LondonO. Driving along the M1, north from London takes you past Sherwood Forest, home of Robin Hood. But to be fair, all motorways/highways are built to get us from one place to another as rapidly as possible with as few distractions as possible. The M4 goes by Stonehenge, but you have to get off the Motorway to see it. The 401 is 817.9 miles long and the Highway 400 going north from Toronto is 226.4 miles long, which is still longer than the longest British Motorway, the M6 which is 225 miles long. The longest national highway in the world is the Trans-Canada which is 4,860 miles (7, 821 km) long, but we're not going there at the moment.

No matter what we say, highways/motorways are boring. Why mention them here? Larry has spent a lot of time on highways. They are the beginnings of new adventures and the stuff of old memories. In his six months back in Canada, he travelled a total of 4,280 miles on Ontario highways, mostly because things worth getting to from LondonO involve a lot of miles (km) and a good car. He doesn't drive in Britain, but has traveled on plenty of motorways. He prefers the train or a coach (bus) there because driving is simply too taxing on British roads. But more of that in the next chapter where we look at Larry's history of travel in all three countries. Autoroutes (highways and motorways) in France are another story entirely. Larry drove on a number of those in France in the 1980s. Irrelevant really, but one great story of Larry's I'll save for the next chapter as well. It involves a rocket launcher.

CHAPTER 3

PLANES, TRAINS, AUTOMOBILES & BOATS: TRAVEL

"Thank God men cannot fly, and lay waste the sky as well as the earth." Henry David Thoreau

Flying. Larry used to look forward to it. Not so much anymore. He still likes the flying, being high in the sky, but not the airplane experience. I say anymore because at one time flying in planes was exciting for Larry. The thrill of the take-off, the inflight movie, being served a meal, the whole package. But as with most things, it wears thin. Not even sure why he took to flying in planes after his first experience.

Larry was 7-years-old, living in Whitby, Ontario. His dad had taken another position selling shoes with another store, not owned by the first, poacher guy. This boss was more amenable. He had a small shoe store in one of those ubiquitous strip plazas on the main drag. This boss owned his own plane, one of those single prop, '58 Cessna 172s. Like most men, he had an eye for Larry's mum. She was a looker and men noticed. He asked Larry's mum to go up with him. She said yes, but he'd have to take her boys too, Larry and his younger brother.

The airport was down the road in Oshawa. Great little airport. Out on the tarmac sat an old Lancaster bomber from the Second World War. Larry recalls it being in pretty good shape. It certainly was to a seven-year-old boy. Best of all, no health and safety back then. Larry and his brother crawled all through that plane pretending to be gunners and pilots, shouting commands to each other. Larry's brother was only five, but held his own on those long, pretend flights over enemy territory, shooting at enemy fighters and dropping bombs willy-nilly. The commands came fast and furious between the crew of two, made all the more incomprehensible because the two young men had half their teeth missing. Every so often, other intrepid lads joined in to beef up the crew. Good times, though dangerous, all those sharp edged gadgets left behind. Somehow we all survived, unlike the many real Lancaster crews who never came back.

The Cessna seemed so tiny after the Lanc visits. The sky was clear the day of the flight. Larry was as apprehensive as he was excited about actually going up into it. He'd rather have stayed in the Lanc. The Cessna eased its way along the tarmac to the runway readying for takeoff. Larry and his brother sat in the back, holding their breaths. Their mum was up front with the shoe man pilot. Larry wondered about this. How could you sell shoes and fly a plane? Conundrums that confounded Larry's young mind and would do for decades to come. Bright as he may have been, connecting dots took him longer than most.

The take-off thrilled and scared Larry at the same time. His brother grinned from ear to ear, a maniacal grin that made Larry even more nervous. Suddenly they were in the air, the ground below disappearing quickly. Larry hadn't breathed since the plane started down the runway. The Cessna eventually levelled off and a very red-faced Larry finally took a breath. The world below was so small. His brother couldn't see much through the plane's window and kept asking Larry what it looked like. Larry described the green fields and the tiny airport below. He could see Lake Ontario and Oshawa open up before him. Tiny toy cars moved along the roads. Everything was so peaceful until the door on his mother's side unexpectedly flew open. The air rushed in and Larry and his brother held their breaths again.

Larry's mum was too stunned to scream. She leaned over and hung on to the pilot's arm. Had he planned the whole thing? The pilot, dad's boss, told us all to hang on. We did. He cut the engine, causing Larry's eyes to bulge in fear, rolled the plane on its side and waited until the door slammed back shut. Took him several attempts to restart the engine. No one breathed. The prop sputtered and then….well, you get the picture. The ride was over and the pilot landed safely. The only casualties were the trousers of two young boys and the cloth on the seats of the Cessna. Larry had thought he would lose his mum that day. A terrifying start to flying.

The next flight came on Larry's 22nd birthday, BOAC from Toronto to his old homeland. He was spoiled from the beginning. He wore a suit and carried himself so well he was offered a first class seat for the trip over. Some elderly woman's husband couldn't make the trip at the last moment and she wanted a seat companion who reminded her of her son. Larry fit the bill. She talked nearly the whole flight. But the food was good and the seat comfortable. His ears felt like exploding on the approach above the Thames to Heathrow. He decided then and there (or there and then….depending from where you hail) that flying may not be his thing. The return flight was in coach. Felt like a stage coach, cramped, noisy and the food was less than desirable, like a box lunch.

So bad was his memory of that day that when he moved from Toronto to Vancouver two years later, he drove instead, all alone, in a spiffy little Fiat Bertone X/19, mid-engine, bored-out motor, Toyo radials, lovely. There and back it took him when he accepted a job in Vancouver and quit within a few months. Larry saw a lot of Canada in four months, four wheels firmly planted on terra firma. Larry liked driving. Especially alone. He was more or less in control of the vehicle and in full command of the entertainment and places to stop. Driving has lost its lustre over the years. Too stressful. Larry says there are more lunatics on the road these days. Everywhere. All countries. He doesn't drive in Britain. When he's back in Canada, he'll rent a car to go places, but prefers walking when and where possible and taking public transport. Still, every time he watches Top Gear Larry drools over cars he might have had. Fortunately, he's skint (broke).

Larry's next trip to England was with his whole family in 1978. They flew. They could have sailed. That's how Larry got to Canada in the first place, aboard the SS Scythia, an immigrant ship. It is often referred to as RMS Scythia II, not sure why. Lots of people left Europe for Canada in the 1950s. Larry's mum and his brother sailed in July of 1955. It was a memorable trip for all the wrong reasons.

Larry had his first encounter with French culture aboard the Scythia. A young French family from Paris headed for Quebec where the ship would dock. Their young son was a little older than Larry. He envied Larry's array of Dinky Toys, small scale metal replicas of cars, buses and army vehicles, and his Golliwog doll. He asked Larry in French if he could play on deck with him. In typical English fashion, not understanding a word and not really wanting to, Larry pushed the boy away.

The next action may have begun an international incident if grownups had been involved. Instead, boys will be boys. The French boy, feeling slighted, grabbed Larry's toys and his Golliwog and ran to the ship's railing, hurling everything into the ocean. Larry let go an English howl and ran after the lad, tripping over the coaming that leads through a door on deck. The French boy escaped. Larry ended up banging his eye on a railing on the other side of the door and had to wear an unsightly patch for the rest of the voyage. There was a consolation. Word got to the captain of the Scythia through a purser whom Larry had begged to stop the ship to search for his toys. The captain invited Larry to ring the ship's bell in memory of his loss. But Larry never forgave the French and that's the one and only time he sailed across an ocean. Cruises be damned.

The trip in 1978, back to England, convinced Larry that one day he wanted to live there. He still loved flying at this point. He visited the old home in East Sheen with his parents and brother. The White Cottage still stood in its place back then. They travelled on the Tube to get to the old homestead. The London Underground is a labrynth, but once you get used to it, you can go anywhere. Larry loved it. Every Tube ride, train excursion, double-decker bus trip, coach tour and even minicab ride was a marvel to behold for Larry. Whenever he thought of England in subsequent years, he thought of green fields, rose gardens and diesel fumes. Why the latter stayed as a good and lasting impression remains a mystery that only Larry could understand but never be able to explain.

That year, his coach trip to Scotland all alone would stay in his memory forever. He was supposed to go with family, but his then sister-in-law got food poisoning the day of the trip to his old homestead and was hospitalised in Lewisham, not quite the dump back then it is today, but close. Larry decided the only thing to do was abandon ship and go on his own. It was an overnight coach from London Victoria to Edinburgh. He didn't sleep much. Four Scottish lads in light-blue Teddy Boy suits with black trimmed jackets and clunky shoes kept him up all night with some of the funniest banter Larry can remember. Everybody they talked about was a 'bampot' and everything they discussed was 'shambolic'.

Larry thought it impertinent to ask what they had been doing in London. They were as intimidating as they were comedic. He just listened and laughed to himself as they tore apart everything from Punk bands to Scottish Footballers, the Royals to horse racing. The coach rattled on mile after mile with only moments of quiet before another explosion of witty banter filled the air. The only other two on the coach seemed oblivious to the goings on and slept the entire journey except once when one of them woke for an instant, rolled his eyes at the proceedings and went back to sleep.

The coach rolled into Edinburgh early in the morning, dropping a weary lot at the train station. Larry booked the next train to Inverness and had a couple of hours to walk about. He chose the Royal mile up to the castle perched on the mount. Unmissable. Past the home of John Knox, the formidable Presbyterian preacher to St. Giles where he preached and on to the castle. A quick look around, back down the mile by bus, to the station and on the train to Inverness. He still had not slept. And he wouldn't on this journey because he wanted to see everything, even as they passed through Aberdeen. When the train stopped at Pitlochry, Larry wanted to get off, the place looked so nice.

In Aberdeen, a very attractive redhead got on the train taking the seat beside Larry. He couldn't believe his luck. They talked all the way to Inverness. Larry can't recall her name, but she told him all about Pitlochry, making it a place he has always wanted to go and see (but as yet has not). She pointed out the different heathers on the hills they passed and told him about things to see in Inverness. "You absolutely must take the coach trip to the end of Loch Ness" she said.

And so he did. The last coach leaving that day to the end of the lake. Departure immediate. Larry ran with his bag flagging the coach as it left the terminal. Still no sleep. He forced himself to stay awake. He'd be staring at some part of the loch willing Nessie to appear when he felt himself drifting into the land of nod. A slap on the face and a sort of coughing noise would bring him to. Back to the sights it was, Urquhart Castle and places that looked grand but of which Larry had no idea what he was viewing. He had no guide book, nor was any guide on the coach as it was a local bus. He only knew Urquhart Castle because he'd seen it in so many movies.

The bus finally got to the end of the lake where Larry had to wait for the ride back. He had a little time and spent it standing at the end of the lake looking out for Nessie while checking back for the bus and watching some school lads playing cricket on the grounds of the Fort Augustus Abbey school. Larry eventually got the bus back to Inverness, but stayed awake to make sure he never forgot anything. He arrived in Inverness and made his way to a B&B run by an eccentric little old English lady. She fussed because Larry had come in late (he had called up to book just before getting the bus to Fort Augustus, a place recommended by the redhead) telling him in no uncertain terms that he'd better not be out late. Larry wandered into town to have a meal with the redhead, who, it turns out, had phoned the place she had recommended, giving the time and place to meet. He told the young woman all about his trip along the loch. She filled in details about things Larry had seen. She was a nurse, coming to Inverness for a week of training of some sort. It got late. She went back to her dormitory and Larry headed back to the B&B and finally went to sleep. I know what you're thinking. I'm thinking the same thing.

The next morning Larry took a train to Glasgow. He found a hotel near the train station, an olde world, dusty, Victorian charm to the place. Probably no longer exists. He went to the bar for a pint and listened to a group of Liverpudlian construction workers arguing with some Glaswegian workers in boiler suits (coveralls) whether or not Billy Connolly was a true Glaswegian. Scintillating. So much so that Larry decided to take a walk before turning in. He had to be back in Edinburgh the next day to catch the coach back to London. He knew nothing of Glasgow and its reputation back then. Especially around the river front. He had never heard of the Gorbals.

Larry blithely pressed on along Clyde Street toward Gorbals Street. A sense of eeriness hung over the place. No one seemed to be about. A ghost town. That is until Larry passed a pub where he heard shouts of anger from within. A moment later a woman came tumbling out the door, head over heels, cursing at the two large men who had tossed her to the pavement (sidewalk). She was bleeding pretty badly from the head and arms, but got up, threw Larry a 'What you looking at, fuck-off' look, screamed something that had to be swearing in Gaelic and ran back into the pub. Larry the Intrepid turned and fled back over the bridge to safety.

He soon discovered why everywhere appeared deserted. Seemingly from nowhere hordes of people festooned in blue or white football jerseys, Scottish football scarves, banners waving, bands playing, bagpipes skirling and people singing and chanting slogans were on their way to see their beloved national football team off to the 1978 World Cup in Argentina beginning at Glasgow's Central train Station. Scotland were the only team to represent Great Britain at this World Cup. Hopes were high, only to be dashed within a few weeks, the team returning with only one victory, that against the eventual finalists, the Dutch. It was quite a raucous night. Larry did not sleep well and missed old LondonE, even Deptford where he was staying with his Nan (grandma).

Deptford, in southeast London where our story takes place (but north of where Larry currently resides and along the Thames) is still every bit the old part of London Larry remembers. But it's changing too. Rapidly. Once it was part of the old London Docks system. Now it is fast becoming the new place to be for young urbanite professionals (the old yuppie bunch). Larry's Nan would be amused. She still had an outdoor toilet in 1978. Deptford was once a Royal Dockyard. King Henry VIII opened it for shipbuilding and the likes of Peter the Great of Russia came to see how ships were built. Pete is responsible for the first ever Russian navy. Larry wishes he hadn't bothered, Russians being what they are today, but that too is another story. Elizabeth I knighted Sir Francis Drake here. Deptford declined as the docks slowly closed over the years. The Second World War saw much of Deptford bombed. Larry's mum had a shelter in the garden, one of the Anderson Shelters as they were called. They weren't much good from a direct hit, but it did the job keeping Larry's mum and family safe. 88 Trundleys Road was a haven for Larry on his two trips to England, and untouched by Hitler.

Trundleys Road saw its share of horror during the war. Just up the street and under the railway bridge is an area called Folkstone Gardens. Nice name for blocks of flats, old Victorian houses and small shops. On a lovely day in

March, 1945, one of Hitler's V2 rocket bombs fell between two of the blocks of flats destroying them, 5 houses nearby and 10 shops. In all, 53 people were killed. The worst hit of the war also took place in Deptford. A V2 slammed into a Woolworths store in New Cross High Street killing 168. Larry's mum was safe in both instances, but she says she and her future husband (Larry's dad) were out for a walk that day and heard and saw the explosion from a safe distance. She and her family had moved from Folkstone Gardens to another house past the railway bridge on Trundleys Road just before the war. Just in time. For Larry's mum anyway. Larry made his way by train back to Edinburgh and caught the coach back to London. All aboard behaved themselves. Boring.

Back in the economic boom days of the late 70s and 80s, even the 90s, airline travel was more amenable. That means in economy seating as well. They didn't have TV screens on the back of every seat, but the food was better and it seemed there was more leg room. Larry's family liked travelling Wardair; cheap, cheerful and accommodating. Those kinds of airlines are gone now, except for the national ones. But you pay a fortune to fly with them (British Airways [BA], Air Canada and Air France to name the few related to this book). Larry would fly Air Transat, the cheaper option these days between Toronto and LondonE, but there is little leg room (he's 6'2"), the entertainment (at time of writing) was still the screen on the bulkhead, the food nasty and the check-in area at LondonE, Gatwick airport is almost hidden down some back alleyway in the terminal.

So, he flies either Air Canada or BA from LondonE Heathrow. A little more leg room, better food (generally) and a TV screen at each seat with plenty of individual viewing options to pass the 8 hour journey more pleasantly....when they're working of course. Even though it takes nearly the same time as the flight to check the baggage, go through security and walk ten miles along countless corridors to the departure gate. With BA, a bus takes you to the plane and you get on the old-fashioned way up the steps. Terminal 5 at Heathrow is a well-equipped barn, cavernous, sprawling and noisy. Don't even get Larry started about Pearson International Airport in Toronto. But at least the moving sidewalks are usually all operating. They have that over the Brits.

In the 1980s, Larry travelled to France and back on Air France. Not bad. But the French can be terribly rude. They once overbooked a flight from Charles DeGaulle Airport in Paris to Toronto and shuffled Larry and his family at the time on to another aircraft to be taken to Amsterdam, transfer to another Air France plane and on to Toronto. The only problem was no Air France plane showed up. As yet, no apologies. When Larry inquired as to the reason for the delay (he had a wife, a child and an infant to worry about) the Air France rep looked at him disdainfully and said Larry and his family were travelling economy and had no right to question her. She told Larry to go and sit down to wait for an announcement. KLM to the rescue. Royal Dutch Airline put on an extra plane for the weary travellers, the best flight Larry had ever been on before that time and to this very day. And he has flown a lot.

Something about seeing the world from 38,000 feet makes the problems of the world diminish. Larry loves it up there. If you could dispense with all the nonsense you have to go through before takeoff and after landing, Larry would prefer to fly even to the local grocery store. That is not likely since to reach 38,000 feet and then drop to the grocery store a half mile away would be senseless. Larry walks instead or catches a B15 bus from around the corner. His only options. Staying in the air would be preferable in a slightly larger object or being in Business Class (they rarely say First Class anymore, it's not PC). After a while, sitting in the rather narrow fuselage with crying kids, farting neighbours and being made to move all the time (Larry prefers aisle seats these days) by weak bladdered types becomes tedious. He used to like the window seats where he could see the world go by, even if most of it was ocean. But he is of the age now when he is the one getting up more often and not only because of his bladder and bowels. A few years ago he read about having to get out of his seat to move around for fear of getting deep vein thrombosis. His feet swell after every flight (don't tell him I told you).

Larry has never yet met an airport he likes. They are ungainly. Heathrow nearly lost his Gibson guitar when he moved to LondonE. He was harassed by one of those officious security checkers in Toronto. She didn't speak English very well and when Larry had asked her to repeat what she asked him because he hadn't understood that he was to remove his belt, she took exception and decided to empty his carry-on bag to examine its contents....meticulously. Nasty that. Spiteful. Don't ever tell Larry that these government employees are neutral and unbiased. Everything on sale at these places is way too expensive. Duty Free is a con. Waiting in line to check bags then waiting forever beside the carousel at the other end to retrieve the same bag (if indeed it has arrived at all) is irritating. You can tell Larry is getting on in years can't you? No patience.

The strangest airport story began in France and ended in Fez, Morocco. Larry was to visit friends in Fez one Christmas a number of years ago. He lived in Marseille at the time, the wackiest city in which Larry has dwelled. That may be for another book. But Larry survived a gun fight, a gangland slaying just up the street, the noisiest neighbours in the world, corrupt football (soccer) team and a sea of thieves the likes of which have yet to be duplicated….and he's been to south Chicago! But I digress. Larry left for Casablanca from Marseille Marignane Airport just before Christmas aboard an Air Maroc (Morocco) flight. The flight had been advertised as direct from Marseille to Casablanca, but when Larry got to the airport, the board had it stopping in Fez where Larry wanted to be.

He asked at the desk if he could change his ticket for Fez. He even offered to waive the refund. But the desk clerk said nothing could be done. Off he went. The plane landed in Fez and Larry thought for once in his life he'd be bold. He marched up to the purser who was seeing the Fez passengers off and told him his story. At first the purser insisted nothing could be done. Larry persisted. Eventually he broke the man down.

"Describe your bags please" he said. "If we can get to them easily you may disembark."

"Thank-you sir….many thanks" Larry said in the Moroccan dialect. The purser was quite impressed.

Nothing for a long moment. Larry was about to give up hope when a baggage handler ran to the foot of the disembarking steps triumphantly holding up a green bag and a blue bag. Larry said those were his and off he got. The rest of the passengers, mostly Moroccan, were incredibly patient, as if this were a regular occurrence. Larry thought, 'What power I've got, holding up a plane for half an hour just for finally being assertive'. His victory was nearly short lived as he was met in the terminal by a very well dressed moustachioed Moroccan man who approached Larry most officiously.

"Welcome To Fez, Morocco" he said in French. Then he changed to impeccable English. "I was wondering why you chose to get off here and not Casablanca. Do you have business here?"

Larry explained the situation very calmly he thought, quite rationally, which for Larry is saying something. Fortunately, the tall, handsome Moroccan secret police officer (Larry had figured that out pretty quickly) seemed to accept his story and without checking any of his bags, told Larry to enjoy his stay, offered a few touristy suggestions, turned on a crisp heal and walked away. Larry breathed again. He decided he would have his ticket changed before returning to Marseille so he could leave from Fez. Apparently, this flight always included Fez, something, Larry thought, he ought to tell the travel agent when he got back to Marseille, which he eventually did and was told it couldn't be done.

Changing the ticket proved ridiculously difficult. He went into the Air Maroc office in Fez and asked for the change. The lady at the desk, a large computer in front of her, took Larry's ticket, looked at it and said, "That's fine sir. No problem. All done." Except she hadn't touched the computer. Larry inquired as to why she had not put it in the computer or changed anything on his ticket. "No problem sir. All done" she repeated. Larry knew something was not right. He'd check again in Casablanca (Casa) when he went there in a few days. It's the capital, he thought, they'll be able to change it. In Casa Larry was told by a very swarthy man that it would be impossible to change in such a short time. Besides, his office was closing for the day, 11am, and he had no time to do it. Larry became frustrated. Next stop Marrakesh. He was losing hope, but he'd try.

Marrakesh is a strange city. Mostly ancient mixed with a little modern. Everything is either business or entertainment and those two overlap. Tourists are a necessary evil and the general feeling is that if you're from the west, you're rich. I doubt it has changed much in the 21st century since Larry was there in the 1980s. He walked into the Air Maroc office and was greeted by a very handsome young Moroccan man dressed to the nines in a beautifully cut suit and a very expensive tie. He spoke perfect English.

"What may I do for you sir?" he enquired with an air of confidence and even a little superiority. Larry explained the situation, including his experiences in the Air Maroc offices in Fez and Casa.

"Ah," he said, "Yes. It is a problem. I was educated in the United States. I know how things work. When the French were here, they ran everything. None of my people were allowed the top jobs or the better jobs. Very few know how to use computers. It is a disaster that will keep us in the Dark Ages for years to come. As for the manager in Casa? He is a lazy buffoon. He will not last much longer in the industry, believe me."

Larry did. He handed over his ticket and within minutes had the new ticket, with refund, in hand. Result. He wished the young man well and headed back into the souks to be hounded by young boys trying to entice him to go with them down dark alleys to buy rugs from carpet dealers. That's another story. When Larry left Fez after Christmas, he ran into the nattily dressed, not so secret, policeman. Larry walked up to him and told him how beautiful his country was and how he had taken his advice on seeing a few sites. The man obviously had forgotten the whole incident and looked at Larry with a bemused expression as if to say, 'Who the hell are you?' Larry has gotten used to that look over the years. He spent New Years with family in LondonE, familiar and normal. He flew BA from Marseille. No mix-ups, no hassles and all in English. Another reason he wanted to live in LondonE one day.

Just when you thought LondonO would be left out, I save the last airplane story for last. When Larry leaves his mum's place in LondonO to go back to LondonE, he usually takes the Robert Q van service. But he hates it because there is little leg room and he always ends up sitting near someone with rancid body odour for the 2½ hour journey to Toronto airport (no, I assure you Larry isn't the one who smells funny). One winter his mum paid for him to take the plane from LondonO airport to Toronto. He was on his way back to LondonE. The drive from Larry's mum's place to LondonO airport is from one end of LondonO to the other, as far as you can go. LondonO International Airport is so named because you can fly to points in the United States and one place in Mexico. Pretentious but justifiable.

Larry's brother drove him there on the day of departure. One thing about the roads in LondonO….straight as an arrow most of the way. One long road gets you nearly there….one very long road 21.3 km long (13.235 miles) and takes about 30 minutes in the early morning when traffic is fairly light. Heathrow airport is 46.5 km (28.9 miles) from Larry's home in Kent (Greater London) and takes around 1 hour and 10 minutes to complete the journey. That is if traffic is moving well and there are none of the usual road closings or hold ups inherent in LondonE driving. Anyway, Larry and his brother arrived in good time for the 45 minute flight. Larry saved a little less than an hour by flying.

The worst flight he had ever experienced. He feared for his life. The aircraft was a prop job, an Air Canada shuttle bus/plane, noisy, cramped and easily tossed in the cold, stormy January air in Ontario. Because of the short trip, the plane flew low enough to stay within the clouds, a box of grey all around the aircraft. Even the eventual and much welcomed landing in Toronto was bumpy. 45 minutes seemed much longer. It was actually 15 minutes longer because of the weather. Larry's plane back to LondonE had to be de-iced before takeoff, always a tense moment. Flying is really and truly for the birds.

Trains are Larry's favourite way to travel. His first encounter with a train was in England when he was a small boy. His mum took singing lessons in those early 50s days. She was part of a musical review group known as The Merry Makers. Larry's brother was left with a sitter but Larry went along this night. No one can remember why. They got to the train station and there it was, a big, shiny green engine, smoke issuing from its stack. Steam engines didn't disappear in England until the early 1960s. Larry's favourite colour ever since has been green. He was 3 years old at the time. He remembers the engine being huge. He has seen pictures since and has visited the Rail Museum in York, England. The ones used in and around London weren't as big as his memory of them. But he was still in love with steam engines and has been ever since.

When Larry, his mum and his brother arrived in Canada, at Montreal, they rode the rails to Toronto. A steam engine led the parade of cars. Before leaving the station, Larry remembers being shunted about as if the train couldn't get started. The problem was the locomotive had caught fire and was being un-hitched and another put in its place. Larry heard the train was on fire from some man looking out the window. In those days, no one thought the train needed evacuating. The world was still a long way from the Health and Safety madness taking over in the 21st Century. Larry looked out the window nearly all the way to Toronto he was so excited. He didn't want to miss a thing. Everything was so new and the wide open spaces were mesmerising. Buildings were far apart, especially for a 4-year-old. Houses looked bigger. Yards and gardens were enormous. Larry thought they had landed in a land of giants. His baby brother slept.

There were to be no more steam engine rides until years later back in England. Larry was now in his late 50s. During a first-time trip to Cornwall, he was looking for things to do and see. Tintagel Castle (mythical birth place of King Arthur) had been high on the list as well as Land's End and a few of the old fishing villages and smuggling dens. On the way there Larry armed himself with brochures listing the sites to see. A model railway was set up in a fishing port named Mevagissey. Just up from the port is an old house containing 30 different trains going through a variety of landscapes including an Alpine resort, a town, the country and a sea port. An outdoor model railway (inside) shows how to make and have one in your own garden. The shop is packed with train stuff. Larry was in paradise.

Growing up, he'd asked for a model train set every Christmas. But his parents said no because all they do is go round and round and that would drive Larry and them crazy (mostly them). He would become bored too quickly and all that good money would be wasted they reasoned. So he got underwear and socks. Larry was determined to have his train set someday. The closest he came for years was a train set (two trains actually) he put up every Christmas, when he had his own children, on a pool table in his basement. A sheet of plywood over the table, the Christmas village set up, plastic trees, a tunnel or two and that sheet of white gauze used as snow. Et voila, Christmas magic. It all came down after the holidays so everyone could have a game of snooker, but it was enough to make Larry content until the next Christmas.

Uncle Ken had the best setup. He was an old railway man from the Havelock, Ontario line of the Canadian Pacific Railway (CPR). In his basement in Guildwood Village (suburb of Toronto), Ken had set up a working replica of his Havelock line. Magnificent. He could switch trains and add one of his special locomotives any time he liked. Uncle Ken was colour blind, so the scenery was perpetually autumn colours, even in winter. He had a house fire scene and a grain loading area, a road accident and a side yard where coal could be dumped. Ken lived into his nineties. Larry thinks trains are good medicine. In England his housemate heard his plea and one Christmas purchased a Great Western

Railway (GWR) Pullman with two locomotives, the second one a yard work-horse engine, both green. Larry was in heaven. He got some plywood and set up on the Conservatory table. He has plans to one day convert the loft (attic) into a train room. Stay tuned.

One brochure for the Cornwall region displayed the picture of an old GWR steam locomotive pulling Pullman cars along a track. It looked like another model. It was, in fact, the real deal. The Bodwin and Wenford Railway is a 13 mile round trip through the lovely Cornwall countryside in Pullman cars pulled, in this case, by engine 5552 of the Great Western Railway. Could it get any better? The whole trip was over all too quickly. Even the weather cooperated that day, fine and sunny with fluffy clouds in the sky. A trip for the ages and such a short one.

Trains in England are many and often. You can get to virtually everywhere by train. You have to look for deals, but in general the price is right. Larry pays nothing for his trips around LondonE. He has a Freedom Pass now (over 60s travel free in London) so the city is his. Every week he explores a new part of town. It never gets old, riding the Southeastern trains into Charing Cross station, seeing Deptford Park and Trundleys Road, looking over toward Canary Wharf, the Canadian white elephant that made good, the Gherkin office tower and the new Walkie-Talkie building that melts cars, Tower Bridge, The Shard (the office tower beside London Bridge station that looks unfinished at the top), the London Eye millennium ferris wheel that may last a millennium, St Paul's Cathedral on the right (approaching Charing Cross) and the Parliament buildings and Big Ben on the left.

And that's just the trip into the city from the south east. Canary Wharf is a city unto itself, a city within a city. Nice restaurants and pubs, living areas, office towers, an underground shopping mall, the lot. Visiting it was a joke between Larry and his youngest daughter for years until they visited there together not long ago. She loved it. The rest of LondonE holds treasures and areas too numerous to mention in this short work. Buy a guide book for a fuller picture. Even then, no one book covers everything. You won't read much about southeast London where Larry lives because most people stick to the city centre (just follow the crowds). But the treasures abound in this part of LondonE. Danson Park is only one of them. Larry thinks he's one too. That remains to be seen.

Back to the trains. Finally a new rail line for very fast trains (Crossrail), is going up to the midlands….to Birmingham, Manchester and eventually to Liverpool. Environmentalists don't like it, but for transportation purposes it makes sense. Larry is ambivalent. He likes fast trains. When he lived in France, the TGV was still relatively new. Rapid trips, so very smooth too, from Paris to Marseille and back the other way made travel pleasurable. The TGV rail system has a safety record second to none after 33 years of service at the time of writing this. The trains look even sleeker these days. Larry remembers them being orange and white. Now they're blue. Everything changes. The urban trains Larry caught while living in Paris were called the RER. His station was Antony and he'd go into the city getting off at Chatelet Les Halles. Then he'd take the Metro to other places. Montreal, Canada has the same system, rubber wheels and all. The Paris Metro (subway, underground/tube) has the distinct smell of urine at every station.

The French attitude is, 'if you gotta go, you gotta go'. Little troughs line the base of the walls to allow urine to run to an escape drain. Larry was told the urine gutters are washed out and sprayed daily, but the pungent smell remains. Pissing in Paris is a pastime of sorts. Larry has seen men walk up to trees in the centre of Paris to relieve themselves. The women, of course, squat. You'd be arrested in LondonO and ridiculed in LondonE. The French are blasé about everything, even sex in public. All in its place. What you mustn't do is bleed on anything. That is the wrong bodily fluid to let escape in public. Larry has never seen the law forbidding it, but he had a nosebleed once on the Champs Elysees. It began pouring onto the trottoir (pavement, sidewalk) and a gendarme (police-man) ran up to him berating him for bleeding in public. Larry showed the man his nose to no avail. The gendarme yelled for him to stop it immediately. It was a health hazard he said. If Larry persisted, he would be arrested. Fortunately for Larry, he was able to stop the bleeding by looking into the sky, nose in the air, a handkerchief in place. Officialdom knows no limits.

Your basic SNCF train from town to town in France was comfortable enough. The French, even more than the British and certainly far exceeding Canadian standards, seemed to value the train for its practical use. The British love their trains but have sold out to foreign conglomerates that have bought up the railway systems and all but run them into the ground. Southeastern Railway in LondonE is owned by the French (naturally), but they don't run it like a French railway. 1066 all over again. The system in Britain is very old and the Brits did nothing to update them. Foreign investment has helped, but profit is the bottom line.

The new Crossrail was sold out to Bombardier, a Canadian Company. The Canadians are simply in love with the automobile thanks to the Yanks and trains are low on the list of priorities when it comes to spending tax dollars. To be fair, there's a lot more territory to cover in Ontario alone. Without a car, people would be severely hampered getting about. The Toronto area does have a Go Train transit system that runs to points north, west and east of the city, double decker carriages as well, but the frequency of trains is nothing like it is in European countries. The cost is formidable in every country. Larry walked a lot until he got his freedom Pass, the only good thing about turning 60 he says.

Via Rail is the only train in and out of LondonO. Unless you catch a train very early in the morning and evening to return, you may as well take a bus (coach) to points outside the land-locked city. Only a couple of express trains go into Toronto. Just another reason why Canadians rely on cars to get them about. Larry wanted to visit a good friend of his in Collingwood, to the north east of LondonO. Problem is, there's no train or bus service direct or even close. He would have had to take a trip into Toronto to transfer north. That's why he would have needed a car. But rental cars aren't cheap. They say they are....$20 a day sounds great until all the other costs are added in, especially the scam they call insurance. The cost of gas (petrol) taken into account makes a trip to Collingwood, Ontario from LondonO an expensive enterprise. Larry had run out of money by then. He could have walked, but it's a 155 miles (249km) trip. Not going to happen any time soon.

Brits are motor car mad. Never mind the size of the place and the narrow roads, Brits love to drive. And they drive fast, that is when there's room. Congestion on the rather small island is a constant irritation for motorists. Still, Brits will queue and queue they do on every road. Only the people who move, sneak in or seek asylum here don't queue, jumping traffic queues with abandon. The locals despise this. Many newcomers don't even bother with drivers' licences or car insurance creating other headaches. LondonE is full of scam artists of all sorts, including the indigenous population. Many locals now have the attitude that if you can't beat them, join them. Chaos ensues. All day traffic reports are full of clogged roads, accidents and road closures. Drivers here have a device on their car radios that breaks into their program to give them traffic problem updates. There seem to be more of those than music.

But Brits love their motors. Old timers still refer to road speeders as one of Britain's road racers, 'Who do you think you are, Stirling Moss?' Larry thinks the Brits have given us the classics in motor cars. The MG sports cars, the Mini, Jaguars, the Rolls Royce, the Bentley, the Aston Martins, Lotus, Triumphs, Land Rover, Morgans and McLarens and Lagondas. Of course they are all under foreign ownership now, but Larry thinks the Brits built the best with all due respect to the Germans, Italians and the Japanese (who just copied everyone else anyway according to Larry). Strange thing is, Larry was a Honda man from the time he left France at the end of the 1980s until he moved to LondonE in 2006.

I have not mentioned other viable forms of getting about in this short chapter; motorcycles (used in Britain to avoid traffic jams and traffic congestion), Vespas (those moped type motorcycles with a 2-stroke engine), bicycles (known as Boris Bikes in LondonE because the incumbent mayor, Boris Johnson, started the craze, setting up bicycle rental ports all over London), Segway PTs (that are slowly, very slowly, catching on) and other boat types like Hovercrafts and Ferries. An aspiring actor friend of Larry's has one of those vintage red Vespas. They are far more acceptable as a mode of transport in Europe than in Canada. This friend tarts up the effect a little by wearing a Steve McQueen motorcycle helmet. Very cool. Larry has very limited experience with motorcycles. To be blunt, they 'scare the shit out of me' he says.

As for other boats and ferries besides the the ocean liner Larry travelled on to get to Canada back in 1955, he has made a few trips. Operating motor boats on the lakes and waterways of Ontario is an example. Water-skiing behind them too. Has yet to try a water jet ski. He has travelled on various water ferries (not the little creatures with wings). The scariest was from Spain to the Spanish enclave of Ceuta. He nearly lost his lunch. Larry has taken several Hovercrafts from Dover, England to Calais, France and back the other way when they were running. The Chunnel all but put them out of business until 2005 when the whole Hover operation including the Catamarans was shut down completely.

The Hovercraft rates the noisiest form of travel Larry has encountered and that includes the sound prop planes make.

Speaking of the Chunnel, Larry had the pleasure of experiencing it first-hand when he arrived in England in 2006. He had research to do on his first book and went to Paris on the Eurostar from Waterloo Station in LondonE (since moved to St Pancras and Ebbsfleet, Kent). If you are claustrophobic, the Chunnel tunnel is not for you. It takes just over 20 minutes at 100 mph (160kmph) to get through the tunnel. Never mind the ear popping, the thought of the English Channel and solid rock above Larry's head made him ever so grateful when the light of day appeared again in France. It's actually cheaper in some instances to fly to Paris from LondonE, but at least with the train you are in the centre of Paris upon arrival at Le Gard Du Nord.

I have saved Larry's story about the rocket launcher to the last. He was living in Marseille at the time, driving one of those Citroen models, not the Deux Chevaux. In Marseille, the driving is very aggressive. At the time, you could get a 15% reduction on car insurance by simply taking an aggressive driving course. It's the only place Larry has lived where you get applauded for cutting someone off on the road….if it's done skilfully. One day he was on one of the autoroutes (highways, motorways) coming into Marseille, the A51, from Aix-En-Provence. Up ahead was an armoured truck, the kind that transports money or other valuables.

All was normal until Larry saw a man in a car a little way behind the armoured truck emerge through the sunroof holding what looked to be a bazooka. It was in fact a rocket launcher. A few tense moments passed. Larry was too mesmerised to slow down or pull over. Suddenly, a flash appeared from the back of the weapon and seconds later the back of the truck flew apart in a wall of flame, scattering debris and cash high into the air and all over the motorway. Larry somehow managed to manoeuvre around the chaos to the front of what was left of the truck, the cab, spinning wildly, but eerily and relatively untouched. He saw that the driver and passenger were intact. Weird, he thought. Behind him now, the scene became chaotic. Cars were stopping on both sides of the autoroute causing more damage, but people were getting out of their cars to grab all the money they could that was floating from heaven.

Larry read later that the perpetrators had guessed wrongly about the force needed to simply blow the doors of the truck to get at the money. How they intended to get at it even then remained a mystery. As far as Larry knows they were never arrested. Never a dull moment on the roads around Marseille. Larry was just glad to get away from the city in one piece after that. He hasn't witnessed anything even as remotely dangerous on the roads since....and doesn't want to thank you very much.

CHAPTER 4

SEX: & MORE SEX

"I don't know the question, but sex is definitely the answer."
Woody Allen

One thing Larry knows about sex, there's lots of it out there and yet never enough. Lots to look at, lots to get involved in, lots to talk about. Everywhere, all the time. Sex. It sells. Everything. Sure, the prudes and religious nuts of the world are forever trying to debunk, derail, demonise, deflate and otherwise destroy sexual desire and behaviour, but it hasn't worked. Larry's Victorian ancestors may have tried to eradicate sex from society, but it just keeps coming back, like a cancer to those opposed, mutating at every turn.

Larry, for one, is glad that sex is still around and in abundance. He doesn't know what to do with it in all its splendour, but he knows he likes it. Maybe a little too much sometimes. Sex has a way of being extremely exhilarating while getting you in trouble at the same time. Though Larry lacks experience in this area, he has a friend who doesn't. He too is an ex-pat who spends his time travelling between England and Canada. We'll call him Randy. Randy told Larry all about his sexual exploits and a survey he did in both countries (nearly), asking men and women he knew and didn't know about their sexual proclivities. Randy also checked various popular porn sights, all for research purposes he hastens to add.

Randy says that since the sixties (the 1960s that is) sexual activity and preferences have been all over the map and back again. Seems people get bored with
one position or one partner or even several partners and crave something different. This has been true down through the ages, of course, but not spoken about
or displayed so openly before. In other ages, sexuality was hidden, practiced in
secret and mostly forbidden (except for procreation) in most places on the earth,
most Western World places at any rate. Christianity saw to that. The dawning of
the Age of Aquarius (though, apparently, it isn't) changed much of that, though
pockets of resistance from various religious factions persist. But who cares about
them at the moment. Let's get back to the ones who like sex.

Randy noticed that more British and Canadian females have opened up sexually in the last few decades. Not all, mind you, and it varies depending where
you are in each country. He says you have to keep in mind that there are more
Bible Belt areas in Canada where the faithful teach their children to abstain from
sex until they are married. Whole far-flung communities can be found in the
vastness of Canada that still adhere to the old ways. Even in southern Ontario,
large communities of Amish Mennonites exist, carrying on the old ways as the
pioneers did, shunning even such things as electricity and other modern con-
veniences. The Amish are buying up land around LondonO, trying to distance
themselves even further from the urban sprawl radiating from Toronto. On a
small island like Britain, people are just naturally falling over each other. The
potential for groping is exponentially greater.

The porn sites give a similar picture. Randy points this out too. He says if
you go on to one very popular site and type in 'British', hundreds, even thousands of pages appear with all types of British women and men having all kinds
of sex. Husbands and wives, swingers, interracial, anal sex, the lot. When he
clicks on 'Canadian', he gets French Canadian women and some men and only
a few pages of them. The rest of Canada is a Bible belt and frowns on its people
having sex on camera and publishing it on the internet. Catholic Quebec encour-
ages it he supposes, sex that is, not porn. But then given the Catholic Church's
record on matters sexual, who knows? They just want people to have French
Canadian Catholic babies. Maybe that's why their women rebel and put it all out
there, so to speak.

But as we know, most porn is a set-up using people in the porn business. Very little of it is just normal folk engaging in sex acts. Few of us want our loved ones or ourselves plastered over the internet in various sexual positions, shown off to the world. That's why Randy asked men and women he knew and didn't know what they were up to in the bedroom or any other room in the house, the shed, other locations and so on. He did a one day survey in the Kensington Market area of Toronto, Canada and the other around Camden Town in LondonE. Ideally, having Larry do a survey in LondonO would have been a better choice, but he was afraid he'd run into someone he knew. Besides, there is nowhere to go in LondonO where talking about sex would elicit a desired response. Except maybe on the university campus, but Larry worried he might be arrested. Besides, it was summertime and most of the students were from some part of the Orient. Larry worried it might be a cultural faux pas to ask such intimate questions, not to mention it wouldn't be very indigenously correct. Best leave the whole matter to Randy who had no trouble in either of his venues to at least ask. Results are something else. But you can be more anonymous in larger places.

Randy made a special identity badge for himself and carried an official look-ing clipboard with actual questionnaires he had made up and printed for the occasions. In LondonE he wore a Hi-Viz vest he borrowed from a mate to look even more authentic. Randy had made sure his questions ranged from the very delicate to as raunchy as possible if an interview got that far. He was confident that he had covered all the bases, even how to approach people with an ice breaker to start. He was ready for anything….almost.

The Toronto session came first. One bright, sunny and very humid day Randy made his way to Kensington Market, quite apprehensive but excited at the same time. Kensington Market is a rather Bohemian section of town presently fighting not to have a Walmart barge into the area. Kensington is a hodgepodge mixture of boutiques, coffee shops, restaurants, small grocery stores and resi-dences. Always a hive of activity. Randy began his foray just off Spadina Avenue. The first people he encountered were around his age, three women out shop-ping. The following is the conversation as Randy remembers it.

"Excuse me ladies," says Randy, "would you have a few moments to do a very brief survey?"

"What's it about?" asks a very well dressed woman in a red blouse and long, black boots.

"Well, it's about sex." Says Randy

"Sex? What kind of sex?" inquires another of the entourage, a quizzically skeptical frown on her face.

"All Kinds, but mostly each person's preferences….what they like and don't like, all that."

"What's the first question?" asked the lady in the red blouse. The third lady seemed happy just to listen and giggle every so often.

"Are you currently actively engaged in sexual behaviour?" Randy stated rather than asked.

"You certainly don't beat around the bush, do you?" said the red bloused lady, "I'm not sure I want to answer that in front of friends."

"I don't mind answering it," said the previously silent one of the trio. "I'll answer it for all three of us. We may seem past it. I for one am active….very active. Keeps me going. Makes me feel alive anyway. Gives me something to talk about. You don't think Ruth's red top is just for fashion, do you? She's always on the prowl. We all are. Not that we get action all the time. But thank God we got rid of our husbands first."

They all laughed, Randy says, as if Pandora's Box had been opened releasing tension and dispensing relief instead of disaster. Randy admits he wasn't sure what to do next. The middle, lady, in a green top came to his rescue.

"What's the next question?" she asked. The others nodded in agreement that they ought to carry on.

"Well, OK. What is your favourite sexual position and why?"

The three were nodding again, but this time in a contemplative way. The silent lady spoke first.

"I like it from behind, when I'm on all fours. You know. Doggy style. Why? Not sure. Feels good I guess."

"For me it's being pleasured by a man's tongue," said the woman in the green top. She sighed when she said it. "Haven't had that for a long time," she added. "Not sure why either. Like Ruth, I just like the way it feels. I think I remember anyhow."

"Me?" said the silent one, "I like it all. Been a while for me too. I miss a man on top and underneath me. I tried it with a few women after my ex and I broke up. That was OK, but I missed men. We mostly prowl and gawk and gossip, but rarely do anything about it. I get worried about diseases and stuff. I guess if I had to pick one though, it would be 69. Why? Best of both worlds? Next question."

Randy said he'd ask them one last question as he wrote their responses on his clip board.

"I was going to ask how many times a week or month you have sex, but I take it's been a while for you."

"Not me!" cried Ruth, a touch of indignation in her voice. "You guys know me. I couldn't last a long time. I meet men and if they're clean, I'll have sex. At least once or twice a week, if not more."

"OK," Randy responded, "I'll write that down. "Now, where is your favourite place to have sex?"

They all answered 'the bedroom'. Ruth added 'in nature', but preferred the bedroom. Very traditional, Randy thought. He thanked the ladies and turned to a middle aged couple passing by. The male of the two told him to "Fuck off" when asked if they would participate in a sex survey. "None of your fucking business." He added.

The rest of the day went 60/40% in terms of negative feedback, the negative being 60%. Canadians seem to be more private than Brits these days, unwilling to divulge details of their sex lives. Except for young people. The only negative responses Randy got from them was to call him a pervert or a dirty-old-man when he asked them if they would answer questions about their sexual activities. One group threatened to call the police. Larry challenged them to do just that. They moved on. Randy was completely out of his comfort zone, but was determined to complete his mission. Just as he was ready to give up, another person or a couple relented to his pleas and agreed to answer his questions, making the effort worthwhile.

Most of the young people willing to cooperate confessed to at least trying anal sex. Randy was surprised at this. He's not sure why. Probably again because he was not comfortable with areas of sexuality not available to him growing up. But then Randy was generally afraid of sex. No one talked about sex in his house when he was a lad, except in a derogatory manner. Fornication was for those without souls, without redemption, the lost of society. They were the types who clung to earthly pleasures instead of seeking the rewards available in an afterlife offered to those who repented of their fleshly ways and sought the truth in Jesus and the church. But this is not about belief, it's about sex and Randy had learned that life is short. He wanted more. More living and more sex. He envied these young people, their openness, their seeking gratification in the moment. He was jealous of their freedom. They were not strapped by old conventions and mythical beliefs. They would shape the future….as long as they kept the ethical side of things based on love and not exploitation. Larry begged me to add that last bit.

Randy wasn't thinking these lofty ideas that day in Kensington Market in Toronto. He just wanted as many sex stories as he could elicit from the ordinary public in a day. A middle aged couple approached. Randy had been rebuffed by so many of this age group, he pretended to look past them. Just as they were going by they stopped. They obviously worked out, both being fit and trim. The man wore a pair of well-cut shorts, a tank-top and flip flops, she wore one of those long, loose summer dresses, slit up one side to the thigh and showing plenty of cleavage. He was dark-haired, slightly receding hair line. She was blonde. Randy couldn't tell if it was real blonde or not. The man looked Randy up and down then inquired,

"You doing a survey or something? Are you the guy doing the sex questions? We were having coffee at the Moonbeam and heard some people talking about a sex survey. That you?"

Randy, overcoming his surprise and slight embarrassment replied, "Uh…. yeah. That's me. Why?"

"We want to take it, me and my wife. Don't know if we're the type you're looking for, but we're up for it."

"Well," Randy said, quite bemused by his good fortune, "there are quite a few very intimate questions about a person's sex life. Are you sure you want to answer all of them?"

"We can take them as they come. Fire away."

"How long have you been married."

So far the man was doing all the talking. He answered, "Together for 35 years, married for 12."

"So, you lived together for 23 years before getting married? Why did you bother getting married then?"

"I don't know. It just seemed time. When do we get to the sex questions?"

"Fine," Randy said, "Do you have foreplay or get right to it?"

The woman finally spoke up, a wry smile on her face. "At first it was lots of foreplay then the act, but in recent years it's straight to it."

"Well, not all the time," he chimed in, "Sometimes we play around during the day and go at it when we get to bed." They looked at each other and laughed.

Randy moved on. "How often do you have sex?"

"What, all the way sex or just blow jobs and stuff?" the man asked.

"All the way sex."

The woman spoke up again, "It depends. Sometimes 5 or six times a week, others maybe only two times."

"That much after 35 years? How do you keep things lively?"

"Lots of games," said the man. "Lots of role playing and we still just dig each other."

The woman added, "It hasn't been easy the whole time. Jack (not his real name) strayed a couple of times, but he knows when you've got steak at home, why settle for the hamburger out there."

"Yeah," said Jack, "I'm lucky she let me back. Damn lucky. We talked about things and Jill (not her real name either) came up with all sorts of ideas to keep things spicy."

Randy asked, "Would you care to give any details? What sorts of spice?"

Jack went on to describe the kind of role play they tried, "The usuals," he said, "A nurse, a secretary, you know. And I'd be the mailman and the horny gardener and all that. We tried different positions, all those Kama Sutra ones and we even tried Tantric Sex. Took a course in that. Better than you think. Jill loved it."

Jill smiled as if to say it was better than the real thing. She added a few more role types and even a few mild S&M ventures, including some really intense spanking. "Yeah," said Jack, "And we tried lots of gadgets, you know, the toys and things. They're lots of fun. Even a little anal. Just a little." They both laughed.

People walking by gave Randy, Jack and Jill a furtive look as if they couldn't or wouldn't believe what they were hearing. One passerby tutted. Jack looked round at the tutterer and boldly said, "You should try it sometime. Good for the old juices." Then they laughed. Good medicine.

Randy asked them, "Do you think you are unusual, a couple in their early 50s being so sexually active?"

"Not these days my friend. You'd be surprised how many people, even ones we know, are into all sorts of wacko sex shit these days. We have friends who are swingers….not us. We tried it once…. Not for us. Some go off to exotic places to have sex in the jungle. Jill had a sex toy party with some lady friends a while ago and she's been to a few others. Lots going on for us oldies…."

"We're not old," Jill said, breaking into Jack's monologue, "We stay in good shape and want to enjoy life for a long time to come. The kids are grown up and on their own. It's our time now. We just don't want to get old and end up like the dribblers in the old folks homes. You can kill me before that happens."

"We love our lives," chimed in Jack, "Takes work, but it's all good. I mean, we have our moments like any other couple, but we bounce back, have a laugh and get on with it. Any more questions?"

"Do you have any?" Randy asked.

"Yeah, OK. So what are you doing with this survey? Who's it for?"

Randy explained it was research for a book a friend of his was writing, about cultural differences and such. As he was explaining things and being queried further by the couple, the sky was growing steadily darker and thunder could be heard in the distance.

"Looks like rain," Jack said, "We'd better move along. Enjoyed this. Thanks. Hope the book turns out good. What's the title going to be? Maybe we'll look for a copy."

Randy told them, thanked them and sent them on their way. It really was getting quite dark. He thought it might be best to get back to where he was staying and go with the information he had gathered during the course of the day. He had no idea what was coming. It was a deluge. Thunder, lightning, rain in sheets. The streets were rivers. Randy had ducked into a Shoppers Drug Mart on College Street to buy an umbrella. It held up for about 5 minutes before giving in to the elements. Fortunately, Randy had his survey papers in a backpack. He was soaked from head to toe when he got back to the place where he had a room. The news for the city was bad. Fires started by lightning, things blown down, basements along College Street (and elsewhere) flooded, roads closed because they were now lakes. Disaster. If Randy had been a religious man, he might have thought someone up there was angry with him for doing his survey. It took the city days to recover. But Randy's survey sheets stayed dry.

The sex survey in LondonE was nearly disastrous. Well, actually, it was. Turns out Camden Town wasn't the best choice. A friend had suggested Soho, but Soho is all about sex and Randy figured he wouldn't get a good cross-section of opinions from that location. Covent Garden was another idea, lots of people all the time. But mostly tourists frequent the area. Camden was chosen for its Bohemian lifestyle and being a market area, kind of like Kensington on steroids. From the Camden Town (home of Bob Cratchit) Tube station all the way up Camden High Street, past Camden Market on the right and its spillover on the left, the many leather wear and souvenir shops, boutiques and pubs, over Regents Canal to the Camden Lock Market, a sprawling maze of artisan stalls and exotic goods from everywhere in the world contained in the old Horse Hospital. The place is a cornucopia of bedazzlement, bohemian bric-a-brac, beer nuts to borscht, buyers' bedlam, bull 'n' cows (cockney for rows/arguments), bamboozlement and bad taste in some cases.

And so our intrepid sex survey expert, fresh from his stint in Kensington Market, Toronto, Ontario, set off on Southeastern Railway from Bexleyheath station back in LondonE one fine October morning. He had his backpack full of pens and two clipboard notebooks (just in case) a thermos of coffee and a snack or two. He also took an umbrella (a very sturdy one). He had learned a valuable lesson in Toronto. At Charing Cross station Randy caught the Northern Line Underground to Camden Town from where he made his way up the High Street to a point just outside Camden Lock Market. He put on his yellow Hi-Viz vest (that's what they do in Britain) and even had a red baseball cap with 'Sex is Fun' embroidered on the front. He won't say who did it for him. Gentlemen do not divulge such things. I'd tell you, but then Randy and I would fall out, not to mention what Larry would have to say. Suffice it to say she was a professional (embroiderer that is). Randy was ready to work. A nervous excitement gripped him. He knew Canadians better than he understood Brits. They are an edgy lot, ready for a good head-banging donnybrook/fisticuffs at the drop of a football. But he'd come this far. Stiff upper lip. Count to ten and away he went.

The problem of language and culture arose once again. Quite quickly. People from every country in Europe flock to the Camden markets. Lots of French and German students, Italians, Spaniards. There are Turks and Russians, all types of Eastern Europeans and one or two Brits. Let's not forget Scandinavian countries....and Americans and Canadians. Oh, and those from the Orient. Did I forget Indians (subcontinent), those from the Middle East, Africans and Aussies? Sorry. Randy was overwhelmed and certainly under-paid. Lots of Germans and Dutch tourists were eager to chat, but that wasn't the point. The two Brits he asked just gave him a disdainful look and walked away. Thus defeated, Randy retreated to a pub up the High Street, a Blues Pub run by Eastern Europeans. Can you feel his confusion? Obviously LondonE isn't sexy enough for Brits.

The LondonE survey flopped badly, incredibly badly. It might have been a roar-ing success had he started out to compare all of Europeans to Canadians, Ontarioans anyway. That just came up as a misspelling. So I went to Google and asked what you call people from Ontario. The answer came back 'boring'. Not nice. Back to sex in Britain. Randy did have some data. He got it from Larry who told him of his nonsex-ual encounters with workmates at the music shop he worked in when he first came to LondonE. They were truly a randy (horny) bunch. Some of the sexual activities in which both the male and female staff engaged (not necessarily together) were right out of one of those Penthouse Forums that Larry had only heard about. Larry noted also that young people on both sides of the ocean were more than willing to tell even their parents about their sexual experiences....in detail. So Brits are a horny, sexy bunch and always have been, relegating the old adage, 'No sex please, we're British' to the annals of some mythical Britain. Even in Victorian times things were raunchy. It's just that Brits hide things better. All that stiff-upper-lip stuff they take pride in.

Randy apologises for the lack of a good English survey about sex. Maybe one day he'll find the right spot on which to conduct it. His best bet would have been The Broadway in Bexleyheath. There's a survey or two going on there every day. But it's too close to home. When all the data is in, though, it shall prove one undeniably potent fact. Sex is not going anywhere anytime soon. It is here to stay in all its forms. How folk choose to use it is a personal choice. In some countries of the world they try to ban many of the sexual acts they deem depraved. But we all know that in many dark, out-of-the-way places in these countries clandestine meetings take place and a good time is had by all.

Larry is very appreciative of all the hard work Randy put into finding out about the sexual proclivities of people on both sides of the ocean. But in the end, he isn't any further ahead in understanding where an entire people are at sexually. Larry says if he'd been Randy, he would have felt embarrassed more often than not. What Larry thinks is that sex is a generational thing. His parents never talked about sex (once again, no sex, please, we're British), whereas young people today talk about their sex lives as easily as the rest of us talk about the weather. And besides, most older people won't tell you what they do in private for all kinds of reasons.

Larry can't imagine ever talking to his mum and dad about his sexual activities. One time his mum asked him if he'd ever kissed a girl. She was not kidding and quite insistent. Larry didn't have the heart to tell the truth, so he said no. Larry was 25 years old at the time. His mother was very relieved. Larry's kids knew about sex long before their old dad had the chance to give the speech. He thinks that's always the way it has been. He says he doesn't know if that means they just know about it or have participated in it. And he doesn't want to know thanks. That's a funny thing. Parents really don't want to hear about their children's sex lives and the kids sure don't want to hear anything their parents do sexually. That, Larry assures me, is most likely true across all three cultures we have discussed here. Maybe less so in France. Larry saw some sights there. But the French have a strange attitude to all things sexual. We've all heard about French men taking on mistresses like the rest of us put on weight. The myth seems to be that the wives tolerate it because it is the way of things. The other myth is that French women are more liberated than the rest. Larry has no statistics supporting any of this. It's just what you read about and hear in the gossipy media.

But the French have some strange ideas about sex. They are open in one way and so closed in another. When Larry lived in Paris, a large Billboard outside his window advertised a morning program on a Paris radio station. The picture was of a full frontal naked man shaving in front of the mirror.….penis and all glaring at passersby. Two weeks later it was a woman. Same view. Very graphic and very public. Then the Channel Four weather lady, very attractive, posed nude for a magazine and was fired. With all the topless and nude beaches in France, you'd wonder. But then the weather lady was from Bordeaux and topless beaches are not allowed in that part of France. They weren't in the 1980s anyway. Crazy morals all the same.

Maybe sex is regional. One thing Larry knows for sure. Sex is as personal as a person's religious beliefs. Unless you are one of those egotistical voyeurs who must expose it all publically, whether from opening your raincoat to an unsuspecting viewer, writing about your sexual exploits or putting them on the internet. You'll never hear or read anything about Larry's sexual activities. He is not the kiss and tell type. He keeps his sexuality to himself and shares it when and where he feels it appropriate. Prudish? Perhaps. But Larry's no prude believe me. It's just he'll never reveal any of his personal sexual liasons. They know who they are.

CHAPTER 5

POLITICS: THE BS OF LIFE

"In politics, stupidity is not a handicap." Napoleon Bonaparte

One thing Larry knows about politics, there's lots of it out there. It's everywhere, all the time. From a relationship of two to entire national governments, politics are the platform from which all decisions emanate. The wider definition of politics is the total complexity of relations between people living in society. And we all live in society. Some form of society. Can't be helped. Some few may try to withdraw, like the guy years ago who bought old buses, buried them underground somewhere in Northern Ontario and lived the hermit's life. Until the press caught up with him. Try living like a hermit in England. Not easy burying a double-decker bus and no place left to put one anyway.

Society has been around for millennia. Thus politics. Larry considers himself apolitical. He really isn't. One minute he's as conservative as any right wing nutter and at others as liberal as Abbie Hoffman. It all depends on the issue. He tends to go left more than right, but even then he is capable of changing horses midstream and more often than not shrugging as if to say, 'who cares'.

Larry admits there are far too many issues to deal with on any given day. They boggle his mind and cause him headaches. Issues create politics and there is no shortage of issues in the 21st Century. Causes and issues keep government lobbyists alive and well, thriving on the needs, wants and desires of the rest of us and their own. Whatever the issue in whatever era, people tend to polarise between extremely conservative and extremely liberal in their points of view. Apolitical Larry (at least he claims he is) rarely takes sides. He's one of those types that listens to the argument from both sides and can't decide the right or wrong in certain matters. He wishes people could meet in the middle, the old compromise, but he knows that too many people are inflexible in their views and stubbornly cling to their ideas.

Larry finds that now he is much older, he doesn't care as much what people think of his views on certain issues. He is pro-abortion, but only in certain cases. He doesn't like the idea that women have abortions just to suit their careers or lifestyles, but he supports their having the choice. He accepts homosexuality as a valid lifestyle, a complete about-face from his earlier, religious days. He refuses to wear ribbons that support causes. He thinks they've had their day. Some causes have been way over publicised and hyped to a state of ludicrousness. He's all for saving the planet, but not going by some fanatical group's methods. He doesn't like fanatics of any ilk. He finds them boring and condescending. Not to mention dangerous. And never, ever ask him to support a cause that involves ice water.

Larry goes on record to say he is not happy with the state of politics in either his Canadian or English homes. He thinks the days of party Politics are finished. He was surprised to discover an ally in Russell Brand, the English actor/comedian (or the other way around). Politicians on both sides of the ocean seem to be more concerned with personal image and personal agendas than serving the public. Service is a dirty word in government circles. Demeaning. Belittling. Ludicrous. Naïve. Larry's uncle worked for both the Federal and Provincial governments in Canada. He said that many well-meaning people have gone into politics in order to change things, become an MP (Member of Parliament) or an MPP (Member of Provincial Parliament) and end up becoming a part of the game being played in the halls of power. Party politics and the sheer weight of peer pressure from decades of inner sanctum traditions thwart any attempt by a mere individual to effect change.

In Britain, as well as in Canada, the latest scandal has been politicians of all parties taking liberties with tax payers' money by abusing personal expenses.

MPs were making bogus claims on housing allowances, travel and even in one case, renting porn movies. Nothing wrong with renting it, just not with Larry's money thanks very much. An incident with a British MP purchasing a duck house for his back garden pond and claiming it as an expense raised the hackles of British tax payers. Lucky ducks is all Larry can say. They were the clear winners in this case. In Canada, it was the Senate that was rocked recently with questionable expense claims. Two former TV personalities decided to pad the expenses. The trouble on both sides of the Atlantic is that these claims were said to be within the guidelines of what is acceptable, loopholes as they are known. Legal but entirely unethical. Integrity, it seems, is for suckers.

We tend to think of Central and South American governments as well as African, Middle Eastern and Far Eastern governments as corrupt. Hell, anyone but us. In fact, the West has produced as many corrupt officials as anywhere. Something happens to people when they acquire power, even at a low level. Politics attract attention seekers and power junkies. You rarely see intelligent, thoughtful, sensitive types go into politics. They'd be eaten alive. Only in a few cases have I seen erudite, ethical people govern. They never get far. They become back-benchers.....American readers can research Parliamentary procedures....or are relegated to the fringes of their parties. Some become independents, engendering very little political influence. Others slave for years in office for the wrong party, never reaching the big office because citizens tend not to vote for socialist governments, suspecting some form of Communism. We all know what the West thinks of that ideology. Deep in the psyche.

Public Politics on both sides of the Atlantic have taken a beating in the last few years. Nothing like a deep recession caused by the greed and reckless gambling by banks and investment speculators to spin a politician's head. Bastardoes, the lot of them, says Larry. Just another fine mess the high rollers have got us into. Governments don't seem to notice until it all goes wrong. And it always does where greed is concerned. Meanwhile, the banditos (not the urban definition of the word....here they are the bad guys) launder money, steal from innocent people and prey on our vices. Bunch of clever dudes (yes, mostly of the male species) who evade the law with such dexterity, provided by the very political framework that has become lax and fat and corrupt. Larry thinks the outlook is bleak. He's not alone.

Politics may have been sexy at one time in Canada. In the 1960s Pierre Elliot Trudeau made politics acceptable among the youth of the country. Larry remembers going to Canada's capital, Ottawa, to Parliament to see Trudeau when he was the Justice Minister. Definition of cool. A rose in his lapel and sandals on his feet and longer hair than the other stuffy MPs. Britain continually lags behind in this area. Sure they had Carnaby Street and The Beatles, but their politicians were as dull as a Sunday afternoon among the Amish. Harold Wilson tried to be cool, but he ended up looking even sillier. The only racy thing post war British politicians were good at was having sex with anyone who wasn't their wives. Canadian politicians have never been sexy, just terribly laid-back. Trudeau might have actually been sexy, but not for long. As with all politicians, the veneer of coolness wears thin once the policies start flying. Canadians remember 'fuddle duddle'. Larry thought that was more funny than cool.

Politics in France are a multi-layered thing. When Larry lived there during the 1980s, the nation moved from right to left politically. Normally, that would mean diddly-squat (nothing) except for name changes. In France everything changes. Made for TV films now featured left-wing heroes, artists and thinkers of past and present instead of the right wing movers and shakers. Marianne, the bare breasted symbol of the French Revolution, faces right on postage stamps when the Right is in power. When Francois Mitterand came to power, Marianne faced left. Serious stuff French Politics.

French politics are more locally driven than federally. The feds look after foreign policy while the locals look after, well, local issues. Going to the Right again and recently back to the middle seems to mean nothing to the French. No matter who comes to power, the French will go on strike at the drop of a hat. If it's even possible, the French are more cynical than the English. You can't really be a cynic to go into politics. Politicians have to be able to put a positive spin on the direst situations, convincing the great unwashed that all is well. If there is negative spin, you'll never hear the party in power delivering it. That's the job of the opposition until they get the power. Then the positive/negative poles reverse.

As I said, Larry has never been particularly political. Certain issues interest him. He tried for the longest time to keep up with the news of the day concerning what governments were doing. He abhors anything involving dictatorship.

The situation in Zimbabwe gets under his skin. How one man can intimidate a whole nation for so long angers Larry. He reminds us of his theory about bullies being allowed to dominate. He hasn't watched the news in months as this is being written. He used to have to keep up when he was a preacher. People demanded that the sermons be relevant for the times. Somehow, people equate news with being relevant when all it does is sensationalise events and appeal to our negative natures. Larry says all news broadcasts are political, in any country. If you don't believe him, watch Fox News in America (Conservative Right), or CTV in Canada (Liberal Left) or ITV in Britain (very pro-Labour Party) or any channel in France (depends who's in power). All the others have political leanings too. Can't help it. Politically motivated humans run the networks.

Larry dabbled in politics only once in his life. He was in Grade 13 in high school ('A' levels in Britain and some form of lycée in France leading to a baccalauréat) and President of the school's Students' Council. Larry may not agree entirely with me here, but I think he actually did it to get out of class. He missed a lot of those. So much so, that his History teacher asked for his name each time Larry attended one of his classes. Larry did a credible job despite everything (according to him). He actually accomplished a few things including getting permission for students to wear blue jeans to school. A big deal in the early 1970s. That year was unique because a number of high schools from Hamilton to Toronto got together uniting student bodies to exert student power over the real powers-that-be, the Establishment (teachers and education administrators). Except there were too many egos at the first meeting and the politically ambitious daughter of Hamilton's mayor at the time. She tried to hijack the meeting to force her own agenda and never stopped until one day, as an MP and Deputy Prime Minister of Canada, she was unceremoniously dumped by a Canadian Prime Minister who could no longer stand her big mouth (figuratively speaking).

It was the one and only Super Students' Council meeting Larry attended. He had more weighty issues to attend to, like girls and fun and other adolescent foolishness. He never again entered the turbulent waters of politics. He said he would leave that to those who craved the attention and lied to control people. Instead, he went into the clergy. Politics by any other name. Refer to the next chapter on Religion.

Larry says you have to include Politics in any kind of book such as this. He didn't want to, but there you are. It goes against Larry's grain. No one really likes politics, not even politicians (even if they say they do....you can't believe even that). Somewhere along the line even politicians have to make decisions. They are usually wrong and risk not being re-elected which is what the politics game is all about, hanging on to power. Unless you're Robert Mugabe, this is not an easy thing to do in a so-called democracy. So, take from this chapter what you will. Or don't and just move to the next chapter. At this point you have no choice anyway.

CHAPTER 6

Religion: More BS (Not Bible Study)

"The trouble with born-again Christians is they are a bigger pain
in the ass the second time around." H. L. Mencken

One thing Larry knows about religion. There's too much of it in the world. Please
don't misunderstand. People can believe what they like as long as they don't
force, coerce or generally cajole others into believing the same thing. Too many
people demand that we follow their path to salvation or at least enlightenment.
Having to be right is a disease, not a badge of honour. So many have died at the
hands of religious zealots. Organised Religion, Larry feels, is insanity on a grand
scale. It doesn't have to be. It's just the way it plays out.

Larry was religious once. It nearly killed him. His religious circle existed
within the Christian milieu. He studied all the other religions and noted that
each one had snippets of wisdom hidden in a sea of nonsense. Religion was
invented, Larry always says, to curb human passions. To rein them in as it were.
Our passionate natures can often get the better of us and may lead us to personal
ruin. Religion gives us a framework in which to live free from the vagaries of
our own destructive desires and natures. The only problem is religious param-
eters are too often bland, colourless and overly restrictive. They promise a better
world than the one we live in, an eternal bliss instead of momentary gratification.

If only we would join them and believe what they tell us to believe, all would be well. Why wouldn't you join? Because Larry doesn't want to, that's why. He'll take his chances with the vagaries, thank you very much. If you need all those rules and regulations, go ahead and sign up. But don't tell Larry he needs them too. He's had enough of them. Give him more Sex and Rock 'N Roll. You can have the drugs, but bring on the good life while it lasts. Don't preach to him. Talk to him. Don't judge him. Listen to him. Don't pity him. Celebrate him. He'll do the same with you and for you.

Larry is aware that his transformation from Christian to nothing is not in synch with the rest of the world. It wasn't an easy choice. If statistics are to be believed, well over 90% of the world's human population believes in some kind of god or gods. This includes people who say they have no official affiliation with an established religion. Larry aligns with none of them, a regular Richard Dawkins without the credentials or the desire to childishly debunk all the different beliefs. He did try, mind you, when he left Christianity, to bring the Church, the Bible and Christian belief to their knees. Not in prayer, but in begging his forgiveness for being so insipid. It didn't work. He ended up with fewer friends and angry Christian apologists telling him he was doomed. They tried desperately to get him back into the fold. He doesn't take rejection very well.

Larry hastens to add that he is quite comfortable with his decision to forego his Christian beliefs. The older he gets, the easier the consequences of his choice become. The further away from the Bible and Jesus he ventures, the sillier the whole thing appears to him. Larry had been, how to put it, steeped in the Christian faith and its wide community of believers for most of his life. He was even one of its ordained preachers for 16 years and a missionary to Muslims for 5 more years before that. Dedicated but doubtful.

But enough about Larry. What about religion in Canada and England at the moment….and France too for that matter? It's hard to say, religion being such a touchy subject. The one constant in all of them is apathy, just as in politics and every other human endeavour. People don't want complicated or detailed systems of belief. Very few care about religious doctrine and dogma. Only the elite want to know what the Bible really means, if much of it can be understood at all. Larry had colleagues while he was in seminary training who argued over every little word in the Bible, making a meal of it. Most of the other sacred writings are so obscurantist that any intelligent discussion about the validity of their message gets lost in translation.

Not to mention any kind of true historical analysis of what are essentially made up stories. Either that or there was a god or gods who did all sorts of miraculous anti-physics stunts in ancient times, eventually leaving people to ponder on these things, make sense of them and hang on to them for dear life even when they knew better. Larry hung on for most of his life until he let go because it no longer made sense and he admitted it. Europe, and England, hung on to their Christian beliefs for centuries until the weariness of history set in and people gave up waiting for a better world to take the place of this one. The one when Jesus is supposed to return to earth riding a white, fiery charger (horse). The English are far more secular minded now, doing good because it's a good thing to do, not because some divine being says they must. Only Islam appears to be able to coerce its followers into staying on the straight and narrow. The religion is growing in England, Canada and France. One reason is because Muslims think the West has lost its way for not doing good or living right (according to them) and many are agreeing obviously. People have not been doing good for goodness sake, not as many as ought to for sure, so society appears to be falling apart and on the brink of disaster. Islam wants to fill the void. Actually, what the fanatics want is world domination. Sharia Law for all. Same old game. You can see why politics gets blurred with religion. Islam does not distinguish between the two.

In Canada, things are a little different religiously speaking. Religion, especially Christianity, is newer and fresher in a country not yet 150 years old. The First Nations had their beliefs long before Larry's kind poured in, but First Nations beliefs have taken a back seat to Christianity and in quite a few cases First Nations people have embraced Christianity. Some of that trend is reversing in these days of shopping cart spirituality. Non First Nations people are exploring Native spiritualities as much as they gobbled up East Asian philosophies and religions. First Nations people are simply going back to their roots. Larry loves the line from a song written by Ian Tyson, 'The Renegade', "Klahaw you mothers, I leave you with your white man. I curse the church that tells us that our fathers were wrong." Says it all really.

But for pioneers living under harsh and lonely conditions, bringing their faith with them kept them going when the winter weather was severe, the crops failed, disease wiped out most of a person's family or some other mishap befell them. They hung on to faith passing it from generation to generation until in many communities, attending church was like going to work or school. You just did it. North America became like a holding tank for dissident Christians. The province of Ontario, known as Upper Canada before 1867, was a haven for strong-minded Protestants from Europe….the Amish, Anabaptists, Quakers, Mennonites (lax Amish types) and others. They ran from persecution to find freedom in order to live their faith and impose it on others. Larry points out that although this may seem a very simplistic way of describing the growth and dissemination of the Christian faith in Ontario, he has seen firsthand its influence and hold on today's citizenry. In many homes in LondonO, and the rest of Ontario, belief is rabid. God's last enclave of Christian soldiers.

Back to Larry. He once worked with a guy who had done time for armed robbery. He continued to pull the occasional job because he said God had told him to rob from the rich to give to the poor, his Christian duty. A modern day Robin Hood. He actually gave away the stolen goods and money to those in need. He said Christ had come to provide for the poor in a miraculous way, while he used what he was good at to do the same. He was brought up in a Bible believing community where he learned his skills and was told it was honouring to God and to Jesus to carry out his work, so long as those being robbed were unharmed. Now *that's* a church with a difference. Still, he was armed. A sawed-off shotgun too (swan-off in Britain). Larry knows this because his friend, in a moment of regret and repentance (he was also high on some substance at the time), brought Larry to his place, gave him the gun and asked Larry to dispose of it for him. Larry did. He knew a guy.

Nobody is as crazy for Christ as Americans south of the Mason-Dixon line, but some in Ontario and even LondonO come close. One of those mega Baptist churches (Fellowship Baptist, very conservative….there are 7 other Baptist churches in LondonO, all claiming to have the corner on truth) is not far from where Larry's mum lives, taking up acres of land and issuing busses (buses) to fetch worshippers and potentials. They even have a ministry to the Chinese in the community. The bigger the better is an American concept eagerly embraced by many duped Canadians. A sign of success and God blessed. Apparently, more Amish people have been moving into the LondonO area. Not sure why. Lots of land about Larry supposes. Larry never got hold of one to ask. There are so many Christian denominations in Canada and, naturally, in LondonO that it is nearly….well, no, it is impossible to come up with any objective overview of faith in LondonO at any given time. Not even Muslims are cut from the same cloth, depending on which stream of Islam they follow. There is the LondonO Muslim Mosque. The name speaks for itself. Nothing is homogeneous anymore. Nowhere.

Larry's story is one of gradual self-discovery. Aren't they all you say. Well, yes, to a degree. But some people never really discover much about themselves because they get locked into a way of thinking that stifles their personal growth. Sometimes we are taught such things and embrace them as our own without thinking. Thinking is dangerous and subversive. Other times it is because we think we have to live to please everyone else. The latter is Larry's story. He figures that's why he was able to hang in there as a man-of-the-cloth for so long and a good missionary and church-goer for the years before. But how he got there is the story of a number of people burned out on religion and looking for the more courageous self-actualisation process. What ultimately turned Larry away from the faith of his birth (his dad became a Christian when Larry was born….the miracle of life and such….no comment here) is the people of faith he encountered in his congregations and many others in the wider church.

Larry was raised a Presbyterian in the Presbyterian Church in Canada, not of Canada mind you, in Canada. Because the real Presbyterians are in Scotland…. the Church of Scotland which is Presbyterian, not in Scotland. You see the difference? And not to be confused with The Presbyterian Church of Scotland which sings only the Psalms. Apparently, God doesn't like non-biblical words sung to Him/Her/It. There are a few different kinds of Presbyterian denominations, but not as many as Baptists. That is quite likely because there are more Baptists in the world than Presbyterians. That's not the case in South Korea, a Presbyterian bastion if ever one existed. Of the 15 million Protestants in South Korea, 9 million are Presbyterian spread over 100 different denominations of

Presbyterianism. Larry says two things about that. First, that's a lot of hood winked Koreans and second, it proves his point that people, even Christians, have to be right.

Larry's Presbyterian experience is mostly Canadian centred and even then confined to the Province of Ontario. The Presbytery of LondonO contains 27 congregations, most of them in the greater LondonO area. Larry has attended only one, his brother's…..for obvious reasons and not very often. But he likes the people there. Two congregations of Larry's branch of Presbyterianism can be found in LondonE, St. Columba's in Knightsbridge and the original church, Crown Court Church of Scotland, Covent Garden. Larry has attended neither.

He began his Presbyterian sojourn in Don Mills, Ontario as a wee lad. When Larry's family was firmly ensconced in Ontario, they moved from Willowdale to Don Mills, a new town created in the mid-1950s in the suburbs of Toronto. Larry's dad says they were Congregationalists, but none of those churches could be found. Their neighbour was a Presbyterian minister, The Reverend Don Collier, who invited Larry's family to his church. They never looked back. Larry's dad became a minister as did his brother (who still is….they have some lively discussions). Presbyterians are known in some circles (usually Evangelical circles) as The Frozen Chosen. Theirs is an austere denomination carrying out every task with decency and good order. They try anyway. If you got this far, you might want to know that Larry only became a Presbyterian minister when he left the mission field. He actually wanted to become a teacher, but was told his age was against him. He decided not to fight the system.

So, he came back from France and went into Knox College, part of the University of Toronto. It's what Larry knew. Familiar. Usually, people say they are called to the ministry by God (Larry told me to use a capital letter 'G' as a sign of respect). One of Larry's colleagues said he actually heard an audible voice telling him to go into the ministry. Larry wonders where he is now. The journey into 16 years of nonsense began. Larry wanted me to name names and do a little character assassination at this point. Congregants are ripe for the picking, but I thought better. Suffice it to say, there are plenty of odd and downright crazy characters in churches all over the place. OK, I'll just tell you about one.

This chap was never a part of Larry's congregation (thankfully), but kept popping up throughout Larry's sojourn as a Presbyterian and beyond. It began back in the days when Larry ran a Coffee House at his dad's church. One Friday Bill (not his real name for obvious reasons) showed up at the Coffee House, as he continued to do over the years in various Presbyterian venues, to 'check-it-out'. He had taken it upon himself to visit every Presbyterian Church in the Toronto area to see what was up. There were other Coffee Houses in other churches and Bill would assess them and give suggestions where he deemed they were needed. The thing is, Bill is barking mad, a total nutter, probably certifiable, but, so far as Larry knows, mostly harmless.

Bill went to every Presbytery meeting (monthly meetings of Presbyterian Churches in certain geographical regions) whether or not he was a delegate and not always to his own Presbytery. The same goes for the annual General Assemblies (look it up if you are really interested....I can't be bothered to explain). Bill would attend even when it wasn't his turn to go. He would try to speak to certain issues but was reminded that he had no voice at these gatherings. The thing about Bill is he is a walking Presbyterian encyclopedia. He knows all the rules, the regulations and proceedings, from the year dot to the present. A potentially fine mind wasted really. He could argue the minutiae of any given topic just for the sake of arguing and, well, showing off. The uncanny trick Bill had up his sleeve was knowing everyone's personal business, their profiles, their dossiers, their comings and goings, everything about every Presbyterian of consequence in Canada (probably about 10,000 of the 410,000 Presbyterians in 2001). Impressive really. But creepy. He'd approach Larry at one of those Presbytery meetings, not having seen him in years, and check his facts about where Larry had been and what he'd been up to during the intervening time. Bill was always correct.

He had a falling out with his minister one day, who was not prepared to put up with Bill's nonsense. He was devastated. But did it deter Bill in any way from gathering facts and bestowing them upon the unsuspecting? Larry decided to reconnect with a few old colleagues from his seminary days recently. Facebook, for all its vagaries and time-wasting qualities, is a good way to keep in touch with people. One of the contacts is a former professor (slightly younger than Larry). And there he was in the comments section....our Bill. The professor in question had recently become the Moderator of the Presbyterian Church in Canada, a prestigious post if you like conducting meetings, travelling and listening to the gripes of old timers. The appointment is for one year. Bill was giving the Moderator sage advice regarding the appointment. Never misses a beat.

In France, Christianity has been waning for centuries. The French like to think that they are in charge of the world, if not the universe. Very practical people with not an ounce of sense, except in matters related to faith. Their collective faith, misguided or not, is in human endeavour and industry. They are self-reliant. Churches are for tourists and monarchists, not for thinking people. And the French love to think. They have produced some of the greatest thinkers. Rene Descartes wrote, "I think, therefore I am", but in French. The French believe anything can be solved by thinking intently on the problem or subject at hand.

Larry lived in Paris in the 1980s. He was a Christian missionary back then, one of the other hiccups in his otherwise self-absorbed life. But Larry loved to think and reason. As a Christian, he questioned everything, but felt duty-bound to defend Christianity with all the intellectual power he could muster. He admits now that he has tended to be an imaginative, creative thinker over his lifetime, interpreting facts and even flights of fancy as if they were real. Some would call it lazy thinking, but Larry vehemently denies it, when he can be bothered. He's a big picture guy you see.

On one occasion in Paris, Larry was introduced to a Greek professor of Astrophysics lecturing at the Sorbonne. He spoke incredibly good English. A mutual friend brought him to Larry's humble digs in Anthony, a banlieue (suburb) in the south of Paris. The apartment was just down the road from The Park De Sceaux. Larry and the Greek prof spoke for hours about the nature of things. At the time, Larry was a Christian apologist and his guest an atheist. Larry had to admit that his own knowledge of things scientific was limited. This day was truly the beginning of his journey away from faith to knowledge. Not that he thought just knowing things made him wise. When the Greek professor had finished his impressive audio diagram of the universe and its mysteries (albeit knowable mysteries), he gave Larry one of those smugly confident, yet not condescending smiles and asked what Larry had to offer him with his insignificant faith.

He laughs when he thinks back on the answer he gave at the time. It seemed legitimate and quite clever, but it was the only answer he could give this erudite man. No good arguing metaphysically for its own sake. The person of Jesus, though quite probably a good man or at least a wiser man than most in his day (certainly slightly more foresighted), offered nothing in the light of a larger, inexplicable universe with its black holes, exploding stars, dark matter and dark energy, billions of galaxies and evolution thrown in to the mix. Larry simply lowered his head, scratched just above his ear and said that the esteemed professor had been talking for hours about all things finite. God dealt with the infinite.

The Greek professor smiled again and said, "Well my friend, that truly is the mystery isn't it? The infinite. Not even I pretend to know much about that. I have theories, but they don't add up to much in the world of academia. But even with mystery, I still cannot see the role of a being that has put all of this into play only to say it is corrupt, so he sends himself into the human mix to die, rise again and make it right as you proposed earlier. I prefer to let it remain a mystery and keep searching without the limitations of religious laws telling me what I can and cannot ask."

This later became Larry's creed. No heaven, no hell. No sin, no salvation. Just life and our fumbling around to explain it when it gets messy. 59% of Brits claim they believe in a personal God, including Muslims, according to the polls. Many more call themselves spiritual without adhering to any one Divine Being. 79% of Canadians say they believe in a personal God or a Divine Spirit. 23.1% of French people say the same thing. Voltaire, the French philosopher once said that one day the Bible would no longer be relevant. The jury is still out on a book that continues to sell better than any other in the world....maybe a little less in recent years though. What does that tell us? Larry says it's because people stubbornly hold on to the past.

Be that as it may, in his little corner of LondonE, the southeast corner in the Borough of Bexley, Larry finds very little faith in a divine being. There are churches about, hanging on to the faithful, but most of the people Larry meets don't have time for 'superstitious nonsense'. Strangely, though, in a crisis the first places to fill up are the religious establishments. But when things get back to normal, people drift away, back into whatever gets them through the day. No one wants to think this life is all there is. That's why new spiritualities or old revamped ones keep rising up. Looking into the infinite to see if there might just be something there, some hope, some rescue maybe, some peaceful place to go to where everything is perfect.

That place for Larry is his little music studio at the bottom of his garden. Heaven on earth. His church. His mantras and scriptures are the lyrics of the songs that have moved him. His hymns are the songs of favourite singers/song-writers. His only conviction is to live well and not waste that hour or two in a church on Sunday mornings. He'd rather go for a good, long walk thank you very much.

CHAPTER 7

CULTURE

"I imagine hell like this: Italian punctuality, German humour and English wine." Peter Ustinov

Culture. Like society, it's everywhere. In fact, it's everywhere society is. Culture is many splendoured things. Even within contained cultures, subcultures exist. And subcultures are to be found within subcultures. It is the way of things. Sometimes there's rhyme and reason, other times they don't make much sense in the greater scheme of things. Culture. What is it? Well it isn't popular when it's taken from one geographical area to another, interfering with the established culture of the location to which it has moved. Tolerant societies grudgingly put up with interloping cultures. Intolerant societies try to marginalise or even kill foreign bodies, like a virus.

I wanted to introduce the whole area of subcultures at this point. You know, the smokers versus non-smokers. It's a war. I'd say the smokers are the subculture. Larry says the non-smokers. The world has tried to rid itself of smokers, but they keep coming back. Non-smokers have had just about every public gathering place taken away from them. They find other places to gather. So, you may convince smokers that the smoke and subsequent tar build up in the lungs is not good for them, but they have to have their nicotine fix. Et voila, electric (vapour) cigarettes….in every flavour. Larry says he saw a billboard advertising the new puffs. One of the flavours is tropical fruit. Tempting. Anyway, now instead of cancerous tumours, smokers may start growing mushrooms on their lungs.

Can't go into all the other subcultures either. The Goths and the Anarchists, the whole drug culture and the criminal culture that goes with it (and without it), Motorcycle gangs (but that comes under criminals too), their counterpart the Police and their subsequent spinoffs (like the Canadian CSIS, Britains MI5 & 6 etc.), weird sex groups (bless them), this and that society (animal protection etc.), UFO abductees and their followers, other cults and strange religious sects, nerds with their video games and comic books, regular people with their video games, alcoholics and any other addicted types....well, just about anyone who isn't Larry.

And that's why Larry doesn't want to say anything about subcultures. He considers himself pretty well mainstream, having lived, more or less, a sheltered life. He doesn't join organisations of any kind anymore since his complete life-changing experience and pretty well stays to himself as much as possible (while a preacher he dabbled in Fire and Rescue, an entire culture unto itself and for another time). Boring? Ostrich-like? I think not. Sensible is more the word I'd use. He has survived it all and at this stage in his life just wants to observe rather than engage. Safer this way he says.

And with all that in mind, let's get back to what Larry understands as culture. I have been told by university professors never to quote a dictionary for word meanings when writing an essay. Meanings are assumed, unless the writer uses it wrongly. Quoting dictionary definitions is just behind quoting magazine articles as anathema. Look that one up if you must. But since this essay is not being graded, allow me to offer a definition for the word culture, the fauna not the flora, as found in The Oxford Modern English version. Quote: **1a** the arts and other manifestations of human intellectual achievement regarded collective-ly. **b** a refined understanding of this: intellectual development . **2** the customs, civilization, and achievements of a particular time or people (studied Chinese culture). **3** improvement by mental or physical training.

Did you get all that? Have you woken up again, or did you just skip over that because you thought you knew it? If any of the above, plough on and take mine and Larry's word for what we think passes for culture. You may have noticed that the example of studying Chinese culture is used in the above definition. How appropriate for our times. It may prove to be one of the most difficult cultures to grasp. Western culture, on the other hand, is quite simply expressed as shallow, greedy, directionless and, well, just plain lost. Being the newest culture on the planet, it has developed all the bad habits of a spoiled child. It wants everything now, thinks it deserves it and will do whatever it takes to get it. Spoiled. The West has, in general, ruined many more ancient cultures too. Wanting play pals, it has invited itself over when not expected or wanted, taken their toys, insisted on its own way at every turn, supplied the others with misguided information and cajoled them into dressing up like it. The West has much to answer for.

Not least of which is Larry's generation's preoccupation with Political Correctness. Maybe this might have been better under Politics, but it seems to Larry and me that this is a cultural phenomenon. Obviously a very conservative backlash to the wanton hooliganism and hedonism of the 1960s through to the 1990s, but stifling all the same. What may have begun as a way to curb human appetites and a perceived self-destructive nature, soon became a ridiculous litany of nonsensical rules and regulations. No one seems to know who started the movement or where it came from, but it is everywhere.

Larry has experienced the effects of it a number of times in Canada and in England. He's sure it's in France too, but it wasn't so much in the 1980s when Larry lived there. Larry thinks that Health and Safety has come from the Political Correct (PC) movement. Larry says as much as we need both health and safety, why do we always take them to the extreme? Children's playgrounds have become mush pits. Larry grew up playing on steel Monkey Bars. Sure he got hurt once in a while, a bruise here and a contusion there, but he knew his limits and was cautious on his own recognisance. No one had to tell him it would hurt if he fell off the Monkey Bars. He just took care not to fall. People are either cautious or they are not. Caution can't be legislated.

Climbing trees has been banned just about everywhere, especially here in the Borough of Bexley. If they catch you climbing one, you can be fined or made to do community work. Even climbing ladders needs a license now. When Larry worked at the music shop at Bluewater, he was told he could not climb a ladder over a certain height to reach some guitars on a high shelf unless he had been qualified. And the ladder had to be up to standard. Workers have to wear Hi-Viz jackets for the simplest task, like cleaning toilets. Wouldn't want to knock a toilet bowl cleaner into the toilet because you didn't see him/her. Larry is one of the most cautious people I know and he thinks many of these rules and regulations are silly.

Larry was shopping one time on The Broadway in Bexleyheath around Easter time. Daffodil badges were being sold to raise money for cancer research. Larry broke down and donated even though he thinks the whole cancer research thing has become big business rather than a vehicle for change. Anyway, the badge had one of those pins that attach the badge to the lapel. Larry asked the woman if she could pin it for him. She said she couldn't for insurance purposes. She might get sued if she stuck Larry by mistake. Larry said he'd sign a waiver, but the woman still refused. Such nonsense. None of this was a part of Britain before America went wild with all its litigation foolishness. Oh we like sheep.

Language, another chapter in this book, figures greatly in the PC vein of things. What you can and cannot say is regulated by someone stupid to be sure. Stores (shops) in Ontario told their employees that they weren't to greet people with 'Merry Christmas' at Christmastime naturally. Instead they were to say 'Happy Holidays' even when people didn't necessarily have any holidays at that time. The thought being that it would offend people who do not celebrate what has essentially been a Christian celebration, although pagans began the whole yuletide thing. Larry isn't a religious guy anymore but please. It's not necessarily the other religious or even non-religious people clamouring to end Christmas. The PC Police are responsible. Thankfully, many employees didn't follow the ban. Larry says they all said 'Merry Christmas' to him. He wishes all types a Happy or a Blessed or a Merry Whatever. If that offends you, he says, go f**k yourself. Larry asked me to spell it that way….so as not to offend anyone.

Forgetting all that, and we have and do, what are the collective accomplishments of Larry's Western cultures in the vaster Western civilisation? When we look back, we can study those of the Chinese, the Japanese, in fact all of the Southeast Asian cultures including the subcontinent of India. Grossly oversimplifying things, they had light and dark moments as do all civilisations, but culturally the legacy is long and colourful. So much so that the West has tried for decades since the 1960s to replicate the philosophical and spiritual elements of

Asian cultures in lifestyles and metaphysical practices. Africa may have been tribal with all the turmoil that can produce, but its cultural background lives in the creativity and talents of its ancestors around the globe. South America had and still has its cruel streaks, but culturally it is rich in music and art. The Incas had their four regions unified. And they have their Machu Picchu. The Aztecs ran Central America rather well, though a tad ruthlessly, and North American tribes respected life in all its forms, teaching our modern cultures how to revere the land and its creatures, as did the Aboriginals of the lands down under. The Middle East and the Mediterranean countries gave us our alphabet, our numbers, an astronomical chart and democracy as well as some pretty cool philosophies.

The rest of us were Goths and Visigoths, Gauls, Picts and Nordic Vikings. In other words, Barbarians. You wonder why there are so many football (soccer) hooligans, British binge drinkers, Teutonic militarists and Celtic stories of blood and guts, look no further than Western Civilisation. Until the Romans came to impose their civilised ways on northern Europe, there was a rabble. Tribes of rabble. We brought down the Roman Empire and plunged Europe into the Dark Ages. Then we went into the rest of the world, colonised them and mostly took their stuff, enslaved their people and stole their ideas, which we bastardised to form psychologies and philosophies that have fucked us up royally (had to be spelled out this time).

Our culture. Well, Larry has had trouble identifying it. He tells me he is lost between cultures without really grasping what he has lost or how he ought to fit in with the culture he's in at the moment. Cultures change depending on how conservative the people act or how liberal they become. Mostly how scared and paranoid they are dictates cultural norms. But many of the foundational tenets remain constant. Art shapes culture. So does climate. And strong leadership, much too often the bullying type unfortunately. Mostly it's the way people agree to behave with each other in any given context. They were formed long ago and we, the descendants, perpetuate the behaviours, depending on where we are.

Larry's parents brought LondonE culture with them when they emigrated to Canada in the mid-1950s. Their post war culture had taught them how to be frugal, how to remain unassuming, what was humorous and how to make sure that where they went they'd find Pickled Onions and Marmite….oh, and good tea. Canada was the obvious choice, being the 'Colonies'. Canadians resented having to send their young men to die in Europe for Britain. They thought the Brits were a stodgy lot who demanded much from the Dominion of Canada and gave little in return. Larry says his dad told him to lose his English accent as soon as possible when he arrived in Canada to fit in and not be British. But things change. The Beatles and the Mersey Beat, The Who, The Rolling Stones and Led Zeppelin changed young Canadian minds to want all things British. Then with a new wave of Italian, Portuguese and Caribbean Islands immigration in the 70s and 80s, attitudes changed again. Now you have to really search for Pickled Onions and Marmite.

Larry feels like a stranger in the land of his birth. He grew up with the English culture his parents brought with them to Canada. But he became Canadianised. The banter is different where he lives in Southeast LondonE. The humour is biting, even though clever. Larry's local baker likes to poke fun at him because of his accent and his slightly awkward manner. LondonE men tend to swagger, as if they are in charge of whatever space they're in. They've learned it from their fathers and so on. Larry figures it's a way of compensating for their common upbringing. They have no time for posh people or the privileged class. That's the dividing line here. It is also what still keeps Britain from moving ahead, this sense that privilege is inherited, not earned. To be someone, the common classes have to swagger and belittle. The better you are at it, the more attention you get and the more you are feared, revered or at least respected by your peers. This separation of classes has formed the culture of England especially. For centuries there have been two classes….three now with the added middle class. Larry says the privileged don't make such a distinction. Most Western cultures have a middle class. The inbetweeners. In England they have tried to rise above the herd. The privileged just sit back, say little and know that they are the ones running things. They just get the inbetweeners to do all the work.

Actually, foreign investment runs the show in England at the moment. Arab princes, Indian and Chinese businessmen, Russian oligarchs, and various consortiums from Europe, America and elsewhere call the shots. Things like the water supply, the airports, the electricity and power supplies, banks (as I write this a Canadian is in charge of the Bank of England) etc. The English say their traditions are being eroded by the influx of foreigners. But it's the culture that is changing. The time honoured cultural pastime of queuing patiently for everything is in danger of falling away under the surge of other cultures that push to be first in line. The English know their place. They have had it drummed and beaten into them. Outsiders do not and run amok. Manners are all but disappearing, pushed aside by a tide of resentment toward the outsiders and a general feeling of no longer being in control of the situation. The English are even being rude toward each other.

The one great English cultural institution that remains is Football, or soccer as it is known in North America. I say this with all due respect to the also-rans, Rugby, Tennis and Cricket. Lawn bowlers....one of Larry's English uncles is an indoor lawn bowler. Mustn't say anything derogatory about this sport. England is well known for its legions of Football hooligans from the decades before the new millennium. Things have settled a bit. There are still outbreaks of violence at Millwall games, but Millwall fans will never change. Part of Larry's family's old stomping grounds before his mum and dad moved to the posher southwest of LondonE. Even with the rowdy incentives taken out of football, the crowds still go, paying crazy prices to see their teams play. It doesn't matter that most of the players aren't English, or even British. It doesn't matter if their team has been relegated from the Premier League to lesser leagues. They go, wearing their scarves and team jerseys, bellowing their particular and peculiar team songs. Even elderly gents behave like children. They never switch team loyalties. They are the true culture of England.

That doesn't mean everyone likes football. But even those who hate the game are knowledgeable about it and everyone is on board when England plays. England hasn't won the World Cup since 1966, but that doesn't stop everyone from hoping. England Expects. The expectations have been dashed in recent years. English teams are weak. Some blame the old boys' network, those running the Football Association. Others site the lack of good player development programs. Most think today's English players are soft, lacking discipline, spoiled boys getting too much money too soon and who underperform and underachieve to have longer, injury-free careers once they reach the top. English team merchandise sells well along with individual team merchandise. Teams keep coming out with different jersey colours to keep sales alive. The whole thing is big business, but the fans ignore this. They also turn a blind eye to the fact that most of the team owners are foreign, mostly American and mostly interested in profit, not the game. There really is very little left of England in the Premier League. The only reason the fans tolerate it is because their teams have done better. Fickleness is found in every culture. People adapt.

Ice hockey is the culture of Canada, for both English and French speaking sides. And they are sides. The two cultures clash regularly. In hockey (I used 'ice' hockey at the outset for those in England who think hockey is played on a field…. what Canadians call 'field hockey') there is no bigger ticket than when Toronto plays Montreal. The newer teams from Western Canada may hate the Eastern teams, it's a regional thing, but the French/English split still wins the prize. The National Hockey League (NHL) boasts 30 teams of which 7 are Canadian based. When Larry was young, there were only 6 teams in all, 2 of them, Toronto and Montreal, in Canada. The Toronto Maple Leafs are the most lucrative franchise in major league hockey. More Leaf fans can be found at games in Los Angeles or Tampa Bay, Florida and Buffalo, New York than local fans. They are known as the Leaf Nation. Larry has even seen Maple Leafs sweaters in LondonE. The folk in LondonO are as likely to support the Detroit Red Wings as they are Toronto. It's a geographical and a jealousy phenomenon. LondonO has its own hockey team, the London Knights, part of the Ontario Hockey League (OHL), one of the junior feeder clubs for the NHL. Ice arenas in Ontario alone are like palaces, shrines even. They are more expensive to run than football pitches (soccer fields), but every town and village has one, at least one, and the cities have several in each borough. Often one arena has 2, 3, even 4 ice pads. These are individual ice surfaces to accommodate so many hockey games at the same time at so many levels from tots to seniors.

The Montreal Canadiens hockey team, spelled with the 'e', not a typo, have fans willing to riot to get their way. Extra police are present when Toronto plays in Montreal. You just never know. Fathers on both sides pass down to sons and yes to some daughters, the hatred for the other team. Hockey in Quebec has an even more rabid fan base than in English Canada. French Canadians are some of the best hockey players in the world. Their athletes are some of the elite in just about every sport.

Larry had never played competitive hockey since his youth. He wouldn't have played then but for his teacher shaming him into it. Everybody played in this village of 400 souls. So should he. Larry was never very good. His parents couldn't afford all the proper gear. They bought him football (American) shoulder pads instead of hockey and shin pads that were too small. Larry was a gangly youth and awkward on the ice. He could run fast but that was it. He was afraid of getting hurt and didn't like looking the fool. Besides that, he was lazy. Skating at a fast pace, thinking as you go, handling a long stick with a short blade to control a hard, black disc on ice were all too much for the transplanted lad. But it was the culture and Larry had to fit in. He tried anyway. Unsuccessfully. He lasted two years then gave it up when he entered high school.

That ended up being the last hockey until he was in his forties, living in another small town, this time with a population of about 1,800 people. He played a lot and even once during a pick-up game against members of a visiting Russian hockey team scored on a future (Russian) NHL goalie. It was a fluke goal, but it counted. This time he had all the right equipment. He drank beer and ate chicken wings after the games and for the very first time in his life felt like he was part of this culture. Larry took up golf too and played baseball on a mixed team (men and women). He belonged. Buying into the local culture does that.

Larry's dad supported Arsenal of the Premier League when he lived in England. Arsenal is a LondonE Football club. They have a crest on their jerseys sporting a canon. They are a north bank of the Thames team known as the Gunners, or Gooners to those on the inside. They have many chants. Larry counted 22 of them, yelled or sung to popular tunes. All the supporters know them. It is a culture within a culture. Each team deploys its own ethos. At present there are 6 LondonE teams in the Premier League. This can change from year to year as teams from the league below are promoted to the Premier League while the ones at the bottom of the Premier League are relegated to the next league down. Confusing.

13 teams from LondonE are eligible for the big league. Larry's cousin supports Charlton Athletic, another LondonE team, who were a strong Premier League team from about 2000 to 2006, but have fallen on hard times and are once again in the lower leagues. It happens. Money talks and some clubs can't

compete on that level. Larry's cousin is a loyal fan. He always goes down with the sinking ship. Most, if not all, do. The Football culture lives on through die-hard fans who even put up with non-English players, non-English owners and Managers (coaches), moving pitches to unpopular places and losing year after year. The English consider football as their game as Canadians consider hockey theirs. Powerful stuff. For those still awake.

Larry loves sport. He's just not very good at it. He loves to watch games at all levels and even gets involved emotionally. More on sport later, a whole chapter in fact. You won't want to miss it. You really can't avoid sports. To love sport is to understand the wider culture of just about any nation, or at least adapt to it. That's not to imply that culture is all about sport. Never. What about all the other collective accomplishments of the three cultures Larry has been a part of and lived in. Erudite people think of the arts, all the arts…. music, painting, theatre, literature, fashion and the rest, whatever they are. The erudite generally dislike sports, a throwback to our Neanderthal days. Only the pure arts will move culture forward pushing evolution onward and upward to new levels. The Literati disdain artists, thinking them Bohemian. Artists deride the literati for their pomposity and high-mindedness. Both further the cause. Too bad they can't work together.

Larry did something he swore he'd never do while in LondonE, he visited the Tate Modern art gallery. His youngest daughter was in LondonE for a weekend on her way to Hungary. She is the world traveller of the family. She'll write about it one day. She has the writer's spirit and skills. She is also a much deeper thinker than Larry. The visit to the Tate Modern was her idea. Larry was thinking more along the lines of that other English cultural pastime, pub crawling. But Larry is nothing if not an old softie, so off to the Tate Modern they went. Larry was prepared to be underwhelmed. Entering the Tate Modern doesn't dispel the gloom. A cavernous, empty tomb awaits. The entire lower level is a wasteland in the old Bankside Power Station, converted into an art museum. Larry thinks the least they could do would be to open up the area for local artists to display their wares, an art market of sorts.

The rest of the area isn't much to look at except for the gift shops they seem to have on every floor. Eventually they arrived at one of the display halls. Larry was willing to sit outside the room and let his daughter roam, but she was having none of that. In he went, expecting to hate the whole thing and ridicule each exhibit for the con it was. We may forgive Larry's abiding skepticism regarding modern art. In 1999 the Tate displayed Tracey Emin's 'My Bed', an art piece that actually made it to the short list for the Turner Prize in 1998. Most people called it 'Unmade Bed'. That's what it was, her unmade bed, littered with stuff she left on and around it after a bout of depression. Larry says he's had beds like that. But this one sold for £2.2 million in July of 2014. It depresses Larry to think about it. You can have his unmade bed for far less.

Larry wasn't prepared for the emotive quality of many of the works he encountered that afternoon at the Tate. Some of the pieces actually moved him. Colours and form spoke to him in a new way. He allowed them to penetrate him rather than criticising them for being unfathomable or just plain silly. A cultural shock to Larry's system. At one point, gazing at a Salvadore Dali painting, he was close to tears. It must be an aging thing. The quiet of the viewing halls could have been another contributing factor. The silence as Larry gazed at the paintings and sculptures in that palace of modernity caused him to reflect on his own life in relation to the art surrounding him. An epiphanous moment for Larry if ever he had one. He returned a couple of months later to catch the Henri Matisse Cut-Outs exhibit before it left the building. A Turner exhibit is due soon. He must see that. He's even considering becoming a member. Wonders truly never cease.

The 1960s, Larry maintains, changed Western culture and shook it to its foundations. It needed shaking. Almost every old, stodgy attitude was transformed and old societal rules and norms, for the moment, were tossed out. The world opened up. The movement eventually led to the collapse of the Berlin Wall and the Soviet Union. The arts moved past old boundaries. Music changed paradigmetrically (Larry's word). It truly was a paradigm shifting time.

Larry remembers listening to his little transistor radio under his pillow at night. He was only 12 years old at the time. He lived in a little village in Ontario, Canada, not really all that far from LondonO. The night he heard The Beatles 'She Loves You' on WBZ from Boston, Larry entered a new world. Two years later they played Bob Dylan's 'Like a Rolling Stone', the longest song ever played on top 40 radio. Larry was now 14 years old and ready to Rock. He picked up a guitar and was never the same again. His parents hated the new music. It was so radically different. The styles changed too, more colours and more patterns. Hair got longer....on males....and mind bending drugs were everywhere. Didn't have to wash much. Love was in the air. Not so much romantic love as the sexual variety, but as Larry says, sexual mores changed for the better. Free love was everywhere. People dropped out and tuned in to the frequencies of the universe, backing away from the old establishment with its 9 to 5 mentality, its Calvanistic work ethic (without any ethic but plenty of materialistic consumerism).

The sharp edge of the movement began to dull around the mid-1970s. People wanted more toys and needed money to get them. Though the spirit of the Age of Aquarius remained, greed superseded it and many rejoined the establishment, but wearing jeans. Larry is particularly proud of the fact that as president of the students' council at his high school, he won the right for students to wear jeans to school. Blue jeans were worn as far back as 17th century France (De Nimes from Nimes thus denim) and in the 19th century during the Gold Rush in California. They became the symbol of the 1960s social revolution. Larry was right in the thick of the battle promoting the garment as proper school attire. He would later work at Levis Strauss in Toronto as a stock boy, a rather sad sub-note to an otherwise promising future.

The only thing social upheavals don't seem to change is the culture of war. For some reason there has to be a war every so many years to boost economies or rid the world of some perceived threat or injustice. Sometimes politicians invent threats to get a war going. They may not even call it war. Korea and Vietnam were policing excursions as has been Afghanistan. Iraq, twice, has been to remove a man from power who threatened to use weapons of mass destruction, only to discover it was all about keeping the oil flowing to the West. There were no weapons of mass destruction. The military is a culture unto itself. Always has been, always will be. The military in Canada, Larry says, is mostly run by French Canadians, or so it seems. If Quebec ever separated from the rest of Canada, they'd take the military with them. Until recently, the Canadian military had little to distinguish its various branches. Everyone wore the same bland uniforms.

As this is being written, Vladimir Putin the Russian president threatens to bring the world to war again because he insists that the Ukraine, independent since August 1991, is really Russian. If the West lets the Ukraine go back to Russia, the sky is the limit for Putin. If this book comes out it means there was no World War III. If it doesn't, the line I'm writing at the moment is redundant. But if not Putin, then someone or somewhere else will continue the culture of war. Humans have to have a good scrap every so often. We fight over everything. It begins with couples fighting, sibling rivalry and branching out to perceived enemies and even among friends.

Larry says he witnessed the same kinds of altercations in LondonO and LondonE. People argue. Then it so often leads to physical violence. Pushing and shoving get it started. It's all just under the surface ready to blow. Not a great commentary on our two cultures. There were riots in parts of LondonE back in 2011, mostly young people, mostly angry with the establishment….again…. and some just for the fun of it. In 2012 riots occurred in LondonO. Restless youth flexing their anarchist muscles, not so much a statement of social rebellion as a drunken opportunity to create chaos. Larry suspects the latter is true for LondonE too.

I asked Larry what he thought had been accomplished culturally in both places in his lifetime.

"Nothin' much," he said. "Maybe a few more silly art projects like the 'Unmade Bed' and the big blue rooster (cockerel) on one of the plinths in Trafalgar Square in LondonE. Everything is either a rehash or a remake or just people trying to bamboozle us with false advertising. More immigration into LondonE has shaped culture only in the way that other cultures do by bringing their same old, same old into the mix. Maybe technology has dictated more changes to the culture, like video games and such. Today's kids will let us know how their culture has changed long after I'm gone. I never play the damned things, so it hasn't affected me.

"It may have affected my son though and maybe even his relationship with me. He loves gaming. He played that 'Call of Duty' while I stayed with him in Toronto. He tried to get me to play, but I couldn't. He's too quick with the controls. He used to try getting me to play NHL hockey or soccer too, when he was younger. That never happened either. Call me a technophobe if you like, but video games aren't for me. I think my son would have liked it if they had been.

"I would definitely say all the new technologies since the last World War are shaping culture radically. The bomb, television, personal computers, mobile (cell) phones have changed the way we do things, but we are still who we were before the wars. We just have more toys and tools to amuse ourselves or destroy ourselves."

"And in LondonO?" I asked.

"London, Ontario? Ha!" he replied. "Probably beer and sports. Kind of defines most Canadians I think. Beer and sports. Canadians have been drinking beer like it's going to be banned. I think Canadians have the dubious distinction of drinking more beer per capita than anywhere else in the world. If I lived in London (O) permanently, I'd end up drinking a lot too. The only true culture comes from the university....so again, more beer and sports. I never saw an art gallery. You go to Toronto for the theatre and culture. There's a very large Muslim population, so I don't think they are drinking too much. And I'm not sure what they do culturally, but it has little to do with the rest of the population. So, well, London (O) is a pretty dry cultural centre. That's my opinion. But then it's in the middle of nowhere, so what do you expect?"

Funny to think that our cultural accomplishments will be judged by our rampant technological output. No wonder there are so many books and movies about machines taking over the world. That's how we see our future? Is the West, and probably the rest of the world, that shallow? Millions of years of evolution for this? Museums full of artifacts and paintings, sculptures, mosaics and the like boasting our cultural prowess, and all we can do to show for it is flick switches and zone out in cyber space? Oh, fuck it anyway, let's go have a pint.

CHAPTER 8

LANGUAGE

"There's a wiye ta siye fings, innit." A neighbour

One thing Larry knows from experience. The learning and use of words are confusing. How, why, when and even where they are used can make the difference between a hug or a fist to the nose. Language differences are easy enough to distinguish between French and English cultures. When Larry lived in France for 5 years in the 1980s, he learned quickly that the sound of the French language is more important to the French than grammar or syntax.

English speaking differences are more difficult, especially where words have the same meaning but are used in different contexts. Some of these have already been pointed out. There are many others. Larry has been rediscovering these while living in England. Every other day he uses an expression in LondonE that only works in LondonO. And vice versa.

No one walks on sidewalks in LondonE. They walk on the pavement. There are no highways, just motorways, although 'The Highwayman' is an English poem from the 18th century. What went wrong? Cars have bonnets, not hoods and boots, not trunks (though to be fair, Brits do say cars too). There are windscreens, not windshields and rear lights not tail lights. Some of those are the picky ones. Thanks to American influence in Britain, Brits are accustomed to North American expressions, but to fit in, Larry has to call his cell phone a mobile and order his Take Away, not Take Out, food by asking for "Fish and Chips twice, please," not "Two orders of Fish and Chips." Backyards are gardens, pacifiers are called dummies, diapers are nappies, strollers are prams, garbage is rubbish, dumpsters are skips, a wrench is a spanner, a shovel is a spade, a store is a shop, swimming pools are swimming baths, instead of having a green thumb you have green fingers for gardening, your hair is your barnet (as in Barnet Fair) and Canadians say, 'death warmed over' while Brits say 'death warmed up' and on and on it goes. It amazes Larry how little he is understood when he uses the not too radically different North American expressions. Locals stare at him bemused, as if he has asked for Poutine or when he asks for cream for his coffee.

The Scene: A local American type Diner (gone now and no wonder) in Bexleyheath, a town in the Borough of Bexley in the southeast of Greater London. The 50s music was a Rockin' in an old style juke box. The décor featured all the right paraphernalia, an old Coca Cola sign, licence plates from different US states, a Route 66 highway sign, pictures of Cadillacs and Elvis Presley. The menu was as American as apple pie, right down to, well, the apple pie. Larry slid across the cushy seat of the old diner booth and ordered coffee from a waitress in a pink Poodle skirt, white blouse and a High School lettered jumper (sweater to North Americans).

The waitress returned with the coffee and a little white porcelain jug filled with milk. Larry asks for cream. He may as well have asked for Poutine. She looked at him as if she'd never heard the word.

"Cream?" she asked incredulously, "You mean spray cream, whipped cream?"

"No," I replied, "I mean coffee cream."

"That's an American thing isn't it?"

"Well no, people have cream in their coffee in lots of countries. And I would have thought in an establishment such as this, an 'American' diner, these things would have been understood."

She continued to stare at Larry. This time it was more for the use of words like establishment and understood, as if a Rhodes Scholar or and Oxford grad had decided to mesmerise her with big words. The young lady stood silent for a moment digesting this perceived slight.

"I'll just pop over to Sainsburys and get some.…. 'cream' then shall I?"

"That would be great. Thanks."

Fortunately, Sainsburys was across the road. For North American readers, Sainsburys is a grocery store chain in Britain. Larry shops there only occasionally because they are pricey. The Poodle skirt wearing server returned, a resigned yet clearly unhappy expression on her face, walked over to Larry and asked if single cream was OK. He said it was. She brought him a small vial of the elixir saying nothing. Such is the way of disgruntled servers all over the British Isles, English or otherwise. This one just happened to be English. Most are from Eastern Europe these days. All would have been left well alone, but as Larry paid his bill he mentioned to the young woman that in a real American diner, there are free coffee refills. She softened a little and told Larry her boss was a cheap bastard who cut corners and wanted to make money rather than having any heart for the diner experience. Larry never went back. Their loss.

The strange thing about language differences is that they are as cultural as they are regional. Dialects abound. Even here in England, language is regional. That's saying something for a small island....well, relatively small. Sometimes it isn't the words themselves as the way they are pronounced. The word something in Manchester and the Midlands sounds more like sommit and in parts of the southeast, something sounds like sumfink. Up north it's soomthin' and around Cornwall you'll hear something else which cannot properly be spelled out even phonetically. Money in Manchester (Midlands) is moonay and in the southeast is rarely referred to as money. They call it dosh, spondulicks, boodle, wonga and a litany of other terms. A score is £20, a pony £25, £50 is a nifty or a bull's eye, £500 is a monkey and £1,000 a bag of sand. Larry doesn't hear the last three very often. Those are more LondonE speak than anywhere else and used mostly by those with a cockney background. More about that soon.

People from Birmingham call teeth, toofs. They say grass and words similar to it like Canadians. Being understood anywhere in the UK depends where you're from. Larry spoke to a chap, a Northerner, a Geordie actually, from the Newcastle area. Larry called up about a heating allowance he was eligible for because he is a person of a certain age. Larry understood nothing the man said and constantly had to ask the functionary to repeat himself. After several attempts at trying to get his point across, the Geordie asked if Larry was American.

"No I'm not," Larry replied emphatically, "I'm English."

"I do apologise," the Geordie said, or something like it, "You don't sound English, you sound American." Again, that was the gist of it as far as Larry could tell. Perhaps quotation marks aren't fair to the chap. He may have said something completely different. But that's what Larry says he heard.

"I spent a lot of time in Canada," Larry replied. "Just because my family decided to emigrate doesn't make me any less English does it?"

One thing that never must happen, I warn the English, is to identify a Canadian as American. As laid back as Canadians may seem, blood boils when they are accused of being American. Reasons for this vary, but the main one is the smug superiority that Americans feel toward Canada and Canadians. A cultural thing in part. Also a bit David and Goliathish. I suppose you could say Canadians have a slight inferiority complex. But they are fiercely proud of their independence from the global bully to the south and don't mind telling anyone who brings up the subject.

Canadians are known for putting the expression eh after any sentence, much like LondonEers saying innit (some derivative of isn't it) at the end of a sentence. Canadians will say, "Nice day eh?" or "So I was goin' along eh and some guy pulls in front of me eh, so I turns my wheel you know eh and I end up goin' ass backwards into the ditch eh." Londoners say things like, "Sit down innit. Take a load off innit. How 'bout a cuppa innit." Canadians also sound like they're asking a question after every statement, the voice rising gradually to the end. "So, I was going to the store? And I met Danny along the way? He tells me he'd go with me? So, I said OK eh?" You get the picture. Americans tell us that Canadians pronounce the ou in words more like an oo. About becomes aboot and house becomes hoose and out becomes oot. "I left the hoose to go oot and aboot." Not quite as obvious as that (Americans tend to exaggerate Canadian foibles.... makes them feel more secure) but there is an inflection when these words are spoken. Larry doesn't have that inflection, but his kids do. He didn't notice it until he moved to LondonE.

When Larry first moved to LondonE, he worked at a music shop at the Bluewater Shopping Centre, Kent, just outside London's sphere of influence. It was the largest mall in Europe at the time. A music shop in a mall is never a good idea, but this being Larry's first job in England, he wasn't going to be choosy. His workmates, males and females, teased him mercilessly because of his accent. They loved to hear him pronounce 'oregano' and 'aluminum' (aluminium in England). In North America, the 'e' is emphasised in the word oregano, in England the 'a'. Larry has never asked a Geordie, a Scouser (Liverpudlian), a Mancunian (Manchester) or a Cornishman (Cornwall) to pronounce either word. He suspects they are the same with their own distinctive accent.

Words express so much that to use them in the wrong context can make the user look stupid or worse. Just ask Larry. Forever putting his foot in his mouth. Once in France he asked a cab driver to take him to the Guerre Du Nord. Larry had not been learning French for very long. The day before he had run to catch a bus laden with bags of groceries. The bus driver miraculously waited for him. Without thinking, Larry looked at the driver and said, "Merci Seigneur," (thank you Lord) instead of "Merci Monsieur." So, the cab driver looks at Larry and says, "La Guerre Du Nord?" "Oui," replies Larry, "Vous savez…..la guerre, toot toot." "Ah, non, Monsieur, la guerre c'est tat,tat,tat,tat. La Gare c'est toot toot." Larry had been saying 'the war' instead of 'the station'. Now you get it. That was amusing, though embarrassing for Larry since his parents were with him and he was trying to show off his prowess in French.

It's even more embarrassing when Larry says something in English to the English and it goes wrong. He can't remember the number of times he has said something or asked something and been stared at as if he had Bees in his brain. It used to happen a lot at his local bakery. No wonder the baker took to humiliating Larry every time he went in to get something. At first Larry didn't know the names of certain baked goods, like YumYums and Belgian Buns, Eccles Cakes and the names for loaves of bread, like a Bloomer. Larry's syntax is awkward in England. In his part of LondonE things are said and put a certain way. It has taken Larry a long time to catch on to the local vernacular. But even then it sounds awkward or wrong if he tries to say it like the locals. He feels more at ease back in Canada. Whether he's in Toronto or LondonO, he is at home in his skin, speaking freely and bantering as Canadians do. Not as clever banter, mind you, but familiar.

No complaints though. It takes time. Larry is used to feeling awkward in new situations. He can put his foot in his mouth anywhere, and has. Embarrassment is a way of life for Larry. His brain jumbles words and his mouth often speaks before the brain is ready. No culture on earth could change that. Not even one of his own making. Language mystifies Larry. Sometimes, in the middle of a sentence he will think of the word he's saying and laugh at it. He had to write out all his sermons and read them. Speaking extemporaneously was a dangerous exercise. Any time he's tried it, he gets so far off topic that it leaves you wondering if there ever was a topic in the first place.

Larry says I ought to mention swearing as a bonafide language of its own, used in all three countries. Most swearing has either sexual or religious connotations. The French have quite a bit of religious swearing going on. Larry never really caught on with French swearing being a Christian missionary in France. He heard words come out of people that sounded rude, but the circles he frequented were full of very righteous (mostly self-righteous) types. Larry's voyage into the blue language (not to be confused with Blues lyrics….which can be blue) really took off when he had his about face from religion. Freedom of speech. Speech that puts everything in perspective, from the stubbing of toes to outrage over any important issue.

Larry's first recollection of swearing (the big words) was back in another rural Ontario village, Grand Valley. His dad was the student minister of the Presbyterian Church in the village at the time. Larry had never sworn, for fear of being instantly disintegrated from above. One day he went to the bank in the village to deposit some money he earned working for a local grocer. As Larry approached the door to the bank, a farmer Larry knew from another congregation (those Liberal United Church folk) was about to enter. He held the door for Larry and said, "Shit before the shovel." Larry was so scandalised that a church person would say such a thing, he didn't stop to think what it meant. Since then the word is used almost as a throw-away. Everyone (except maybe Baptists and Pentecostals) uses it without a thought. Times change. Not for everyone, but at least for most of us.

When Larry left the church, he used words he thought would never come out of his mouth and felt good about it. He knew most them, just never used them. He soon became an expert. He was 'f'ing this and 'f'ing that all over the place and feeling pretty good at finally letting loose. The new people he associated with didn't seem to mind. In fact, they encouraged it. Making up for lost time. There was one word he never used. The 'c' word. No, not crazy or even cocksucker. The latter is a good one though. Canadians use that quite a bit. You don't hear it much in LondonE. But the 'c' word is used all over the place in England. They love it. They use it like Canadians use the 'f' word.

Larry asked me not to spell it out. His mum may hear about the book and he doesn't want her to think her darling eldest would even think such a thing, let alone spell it out. If you don't know what the word spells, better to leave it. But it's associated with a part of the female anatomy. Other words are used for it, just as there are many words for penis. But the 'c' word is grittier. And visceral. Canadian women feel affronted by the word. English women use it to stress a point. Television programs that push the boundaries of morality use the word sparingly but more often these days. And that's all Larry wants to tell us about any of that.

What Larry really wishes is that he spoke the language of his ancestors. No, not Celtic/Gaelic, although he even gave Gaelic a go once when he was going through his Celtic phase. Still a preacher at the time, he started to explore Celtic spirituality and soon became mired in Celtic myth and legend, the stuff of Fionn Mac Cumhaill (Finn McCool), Drogh –Yantagh, Tewdrig (Tyrant of Treheyl) and the lot. Cornish legends, Irish stories, Welsh tales, Scottish lore and the rest. Fairies and goblins, giants and wood nymphs are the stories that began turning Larry's head away from the Christian myths of his youth, feeding him with an imaginative world of temptation, powerful love, sex, loyalty, betrayal and some pretty cool scenery. But it turns out, even if that were the language of his relations from a time shrouded in myth, mystery, mysticism and lost birth registries, Larry's language is first and foremost Cockney.

The part of LondonE, the southeast, from which Larry's people hail is as close to the East End as you can get, but on the other side of the River Thames in relation to the Bow Bells. Deptford is as Cockney as any East Ender town, Bethnal Green, Stepney, Shoreditch, Bow itself and so on. It all gets a bit confusing from here because whereas Larry's home is technically a part of southeast

LondonE, it is more a part of the Borough of Bexley in the County of Kent, with a Dartford postal code. You'd have to visit Larry to see how it all works out. The main thing here is his ancestors used the Cockney rhyme that has lost some of its relevance and use if not its charm. London's East End today is mostly made up people from other countries. A walk around those old towns will show you the changes. When you look up at the street sign announcing the famous Brick Lane, underneath is the same in Bengali script and the area is known as Banglatown. Strangely enough, much of the place is quickly becoming the new young professionals' place of choice. Everything changes.

Larry bought a book on the Cockney Dialect by Kate Sanderson, known to some of Larry's relatives. Actually, Larry has two books, the other he picked up in Rochester, Kent, 'Rhyming Cockney Slang'. Between the two, he has a pretty good idea what his people were all about. Mostly it began as an alternative language used by smugglers and dock workers to fool the authorities. Like code. You say one thing to mean another. So, if I referred to someone as a Noah's Ark, I'd be calling him a nark, a police informer. My King Lear's are my ears. When I go to the Joan of Arc, I'm at the park. If I'm Harry Tate, I'm late. Going up the Frog 'n Toad is a road, not the name of a pub. And when I use the word apple, it can mean all kinds of things....apples 'n' pears are stairs, apple core is a score or twenty, apple peeling is a feeling, your apple pips are your lips, an apple tart's your heart and if it's apples 'n' rice, it's nice. Larry's favourite is apple fritter, a pint of bitter (beer). Yes, it's the warm beer that Americans say the English drink. You can get cold beer too in case you're wondering. Apple Fritter is an acquired taste, a refined taste.

Anyway, you get the idea. Not one of the rhyming words is obvious. I may guess that a carving knife is the wife or even more obvious, the trouble and strife being the wife or if you're cut and carried you're married. But who would guess that fife and drum means bum or an elephant's trunk is a drunk or a dog and bone is a phone? The most difficult part of deciphering the code occurs when only part of the phrase is used and not the rhyming word. So, if I say I'm going to have a butcher's hook, I mean to have a look but most people just say they'll have a butcher's. When someone calls you 'me old Dutch' or 'me old China', they're calling you their mate (as in friend, not spouse). The full phrases are Dutch plate and China plate. Now you get it. Now then, give me a drink of fisherman's. No? Fisherman's Daughter? Not yet? Some of you have it. All shall be revealed soon. Too bad much of the language is lost in time and only some of the older ones remember and use any of it. Gradually the old traditions fade away and are forgotten or confined to a few little books preserving them. Such a shame.

The other language anomaly is the use of the letter 'f' in place of other consonants, especially the combination of 'th'. Thirty changes to Firty. Birthday becomes birfday. Larry's cousins taught him a phrase to say, 'Fawty fahzen fevvahs on a frush's froat'. That's how his relatives would say 'Forty thousand feathers on a thrush's (a bird) throat', if anyone were to say such a thing. The point is, when Cockneys talk like that they are difficult to understand. By now you've noticed they also put in the letter 'v' in place of some consonants, usually the 'th'. Mother is muvva ('r's are dropped as well), brother is bruvva, father is fahvva and words like bother become bovva, another is anuvva and so on. The 'h' is aspirated to 'haytch'. When spelling a word like happy, they spell it, haytch a p p y. But when they say it, the 'h' is dropped altogether and becomes 'appy'.

One of Larry's guitar students wished him 'Appy Beuf-die' one year. Larry couldn't resist. He asked her to spell it. The lass was 12 years old at the time. She said, "Haytch Aye p p y B aye r t haytch d aye y." Larry asked what happened to the 'h' at the beginning of Happy and why she pronounced Birthday with an 'f' when she spelled it with a 'th'. She looked at Larry, blinked a couple of times to silently ask what planet he was from and replied, "Just get over it Larry. Don't lose your barnet over it." Feisty little fing. BTW (Twit speak again), barnet is short for Barnet Fair….hair.

Giving Larry a drink of fisherman's? You are much cleverer than I thought. Water, naturally. Larry made up his own Cockney phrase in honour of his ancestors from Deptford. He uses it when no other word fits the situation. With all due respect to the Royal family and apologies to any die-hard Royalists out there, he bases it on the names of Camilla and Charles, the Princess and Prince of Wales, among other titles. Larry has shortened the names, making them more familiar and Cockneyfied….Cam 'n' Chuck….you figure it out.

CHAPTER 9

HUMOUR/HUMOR

"Laugh and the world laughs with you." Except maybe in
Germany, Holland and Japan.

I wish I could say humour is everywhere. Humour is found everywhere, but is sadly lacking in so many areas, sex not being one of them. Humour comes in so many guises that writing a short chapter on it seems ludicrous. Not so if we compare the humour of Europe to North America. North American humour is fairly homogenous (look at any television sitcom for example). European humour is all over the map. Larry thinks so anyway. Depends on the culture.

The English don't think the Germans have any sense of humour, at least not one that is spontaneous and enables them to laugh at themselves. Germans think English humour is silly and far too self-critical. The French laugh at everyone except themselves. As for the rest of Europe, people find certain aspects of life funny. Everyone laughs at slapstick. Not all forms of it and not everyone, but most. We all laugh at things that are different. Clowns are different. They're funny. But again, not to everyone. Some people are very afraid of clowns. There are those who seem to have no sense of humour at all. We all know them. The living grim. Accountants, tax people and such. Nothing is a laughing matter to them. They don't get it. They don't really want to get it. The worst offenders are those who find it humorous to torture others verbally and physically. They're called bullies. The world is full of them. They laugh at other peoples' expense.

Larry thinks everything is funny. He means, I think, that everything has a humorous side to it. When he was a preacher, and a damned fine one at that, he often found himself chuckling at funerals he officiated for many reasons. Usually it was a grim humour shared between the funeral directors and Larry. Sometimes it may have been at the comical sight of folk pretending to look sad when all they wanted to do was get out of the funeral home or the church and start partying. In one small town he lived in, one of the residents ran the local museum (not that the town really needed one). He attended nearly every funeral, believing every family in the town was a potential supporter of his pet project. Usually at funerals, the family asks for any donations to go to a charity or service dear to the departed or having to do with the cause of the departed's death. The Heart and Stroke Foundation, Alzheimer's, or Cancer Research and so on. This chap always donated to his museum and always the same amount. All donations are tax deductible. Now that's an occasion on which to laugh. And Larry and the funeral directors did. Every time.

Larry notes that in every culture with which he has had contact, people love to laugh, play jokes on each other and poke fun. Even Germans, the Dutch and the Japanese. As a missionary to Muslims, Larry noted the best way to communicate was with humour. He used his own weaknesses to poke fun at himself, making people laugh. All the best comedians do the same. Wear your heart on your sleeve and all but the heartless laugh at your foibles with you. Even the cruel at least satirise each other. Sarcasm and satire are English institutions. Canadians can do it, but they only go so far. Brits go all the way. Terribly funny, but at a price. Comedians in Britain mock everything and everyone and they do it well. Occasionally, they get in trouble. Russell Brand and Jonathon Ross 'took the mickey' (a great British expression) out of Andrew Sachs (Manuel of Fawlty Towers fame). Actually, they got to him through trashing his granddaughter. They phoned his house and left the offending messages on Sach's answering machine. Sachs didn't see the humour in the radio broadcast and had Ross fired from the BBC and Brand publically admonished. In the end, the protagonists came out on top. They usually do in Britain.

Larry has been at the butt end of mocking banter while living in LondonE. His local baker loves to gets his digs in about Larry being Canadian. His jibes are predicated on ignorance and half-truths, but they are quite funny. Something about the way Larry says croissants triggered the need for the baker, who has a French surname, to kid Larry about being French Canadian. For some reason the baker knows about the whole pea soup thing and asks Larry if he wants some pea soup every time he goes in, only to add they're fresh out. Funny, but irritating. He enjoys it more when the baker banters with other customers. Always amusing.

Larry loves the pub banter. He eavesdrops frequently to pick up new material. Clever stuff. TV shows panning the latest news and witty shows featuring the brains of the day, all using cutting-edge humour, are only allowed on after the watershed time of 9pm. That's when all good children ought to be in bed. The humour and language turns raunchy. Larry loves it. His favourite show is 8 out of 10 Cats, a satirical look at the week's news. Mock the Week is a good one too. Mostly comedians fill the panel with a celebrity or two from other programs thrown in. Sometimes they add an airhead celebrity to deliberately mock him or her. All done in a cacophony of accents and great jokes. Brilliant.

English humour surrounded Larry as he grew up in Canada. Fortunately, there were enough Brits working for the Canadian Broadcasting Corporation (CBC) back in the 1950s to air The Goon Show, a British Broadcasting Corporation (BBC) feature starring Spike Milligan, Peter Sellers and Harry Secombe (Neddy Seagoon). Every week Larry and his family gathered around their small radio and listened to Neddy try to get out of another fine mess he found himself in. Hercules Grytpype Thynne (Sellers) and his French sidekick, Count Jim Knees Moriarty (Milligan) are the protagonists. They generally try to get Neddy Seagoon into trouble. A host of characters add to the mayhem, all voiced by Sellers and Milligan as well as guests and other regulars. Larry's favourite characters are Eccles (Milligan) and Bluebottle (Sellers). Don't ask why. They must be heard to understand it.

Monty Python's Flying Circus is next. British humour at its best. Zany, mad, offbeat and often unpredictable. Larry wasn't allowed to watch it on TV when it first came on the tele in Canada. His dad, the preacher, thought it too rude.

Too much sex. No sex, please, we're British and all that raising its ugly head once again. Larry missed out on most of Monty Python until the film 'And Now For Something Completely Different' was rereleased in Canada in 1974. He saw it with his dad and suddenly they were both hooked. An unusual but timely bond. Strange but true.

The mid 1970s produced Fawlty Towers. Former Python, John Cleese in charge there. Since then, there have been a number of humorous programs produced. The hope is that the times don't get too politically correct and try to stifle all the edgy material. That would be a real shame. A tragedy really. Cerebrally based humour must never die. If it ever did, the human species would cease to exist. Larry's prediction.

Canadian humour is a mixture of British sarcasm and wit and American slapstick. Physical humour is big in Canada. That's what Larry says. People laugh out loud when someone falls down or throws a pie in the face of someone else. Mosh Pit humour. They laugh at that in England too, but only when the pie is meant to ridicule or embarrass. In Canada, it's the act itself that's funny. Canadians are professional practical jokers. They pull pranks on friends or anyone who might fall for what is considered the obvious. Larry detests practical jokes. He's had a few pulled on him in his time and hates it. Very often pain is involved and Larry can't take it. Doesn't like any of it really.

Larry recalls a practical joke that went very wrong. A long time ago he lived in a very small town in Ontario, Canada. Everyone knew everyone else and his or her business. Strangers coming to town were scrutinised and shunned if found wanting. On one occasion, a swarthy, foreign man (we guessed Italian) in a white suit and white fedora was visiting a certain house in town. The visits became regular. The woman who lived there was a single mother. He drove a large, white Cadillac Eldorado. In a rural community, this was like a hostile alien visiting earth in a sleek space ship. You can imagine the stories that went around about him....mafia, pimp, gigolo, debt collector. Larry never did find out. One Halloween the man was visiting, the white Eldorado parked across the street from the woman's house. There was nothing on this side of the street, just a pit that led to the back of the stores (shops) on Main Street. The house was dark. No lights, no lit pumpkins, no sign of life at all. Our young imaginations went wild.

Larry was trick 'r treating with a group of friends. They were just passing the house when a bunch of older boys and even a couple of the local men surrounding the Eldorado called over to Larry and his little gang. They told Larry & Co they wanted to teach the unwanted visitor, the alien, a lesson by playing a practical joke on him. But no one was ever to say anything, leaving people to believe ghosts and goblins had done the deed. They wanted to lift the car and have it face the house, blocking the road. Larry and his friends thought that would be fun and funny. But something went terribly wrong. Instead of lifting the car, it got pushed over the lip of the pit and down she went, rolling over about 5 times before coming to rest on its roof. The gang scattered. Quickly.

Nothing was ever said. The local paper didn't report it. No police ever came to Larry's door with enquiries. The car was gone the next morning. No one ever saw the man in the white suit again. The woman moved not long after. As far as Larry knows, no one has confessed to being part of the incident. He'd like to add that including the story in this book is not a confession. Once you've read this, forget it.

What Larry finds truly funny is laughing at people who make fun of themselves. Pointing out the foibles of life in even the smallest things, like going shopping, travelling, getting your hair cut or just living day to day. Some comedians have the knack of seeing the silly in everything. Britain has more than its share of such comics. So does Canada. His favourites in England are Sean Lock, Micky Flanagan the cockney with an Irish name and Russell Brand (for his quick wit and incisive views on news events). In Canada he likes Rick Mercer, Russell Peters and Jim Carrey. A friend of Carrey's once told Larry that if you ever see Carrey doing stand-up, ask him to impersonate Charles Bronson ordering a Big Mac and see what happens. Larry says he hasn't had the opportunity as yet.

One thing Larry has observed while living in LondonE is how unforced English humour tends to be. The banter flows freely, the jokes come easy and fast. This is as true among ordinary folk as it is with the celebrities. The English are naturally comic for the most part. Like breathing. Especially the masses that have not grown up privileged. Humour became a way of sticking it to the toffee-nosed elite. English humour pokes fun at everything and everyone. No one is exempt, not even Jesus Christ. In more recent years perhaps any jokes about anything to do with Islam have been avoided and that's only because most Muslims can't laugh at themselves and especially not their prophet. But nothing else is left unscathed. Rowen Atkinson of Mr. Bean and Black Adder fame recently came under fire from the privileged conservatives and perhaps some Anglicans when he posed as the Archbishop of Canterbury, poking fun at him. Most of us laughed.

Canadians, on the other hand, sometimes force comedic situations. Few Canadian sitcoms ever really made a splash. The best in years have been The Red Green Show and Corner Gas. Many Canadians just don't get it. You can't banter with them like the English do for fear of offending or upsetting them. Friends may banter some among themselves, but the Brits do it to anyone, including total strangers. The best Canadian humour is more regional than anything. The all-time champs are the Newfoundlanders (Newfies) who haven't been Canadian all that long anyway. Most of the top Canadian humourists end up going to America. There's a larger audience to the south, over 10 times as many people. Easier to find your niche. Canadians can be funny, but not, it appears on their own turf. After all, Second City had to move to America. Most often, it appears, Canadians can only be funny in Montreal. That is funny.

Larry says he knows one thing for sure. People love to laugh. So, who gets the last laugh, Canadians or the English? I suppose it depends in which of the two countries Larry finally meets his demise.

CHAPTER 10

FOOD

'The way to a man's heart is through his stomach' (Confucius)

Another thing Larry knows. Like religion, there's far too much food available in developed countries. That means food is not plentiful everywhere for everyone. The latest stats I could find tell me that 1 in 7 people in the world goes to bed underfed or not fed at all. By 2050 the earth will have to produce 60% more food for the growing population. With ground being ploughed under for other developments in all countries, that doesn't leave enough land to grow the necessary ingredients for food. Scientists have made a beef patty in a petri dish which costs far too much money to produce, but that might have to be the way of the future. Not very appetising really. But let's not get too maudlin. Canada, England and France have no food shortages. There may be those living in developed countries that don't have access to the excess, but this is neither a United Nations report nor is it an attempt to point out the huge gap between haves and have-nots. I present to you a middle class look at things as Larry has known them all his life.

When Larry was a younger man, he worked for a company that imported gourmet housewares for fancy cooking. His was the first company in Canada to carry the Cuisinart kitchen machine. He once worked with Julia Child and Mme. Benoit when they came to Toronto, learning how to use the machine effectively. Larry was preparing to go to France to study for a Cordon Bleu, but fate intervened. He headed west instead to work in Vancouver. Once upon a time he could make a soufflé and almost had success with his baked Alaska, but therein lays Larry's fateful tale leading to his eventual downfall as potentially one of the world's leading chefs. Actually, he couldn't be bothered and has a hard time boiling potatoes these days. Poor sod. He'd rather have someone else cook.

Larry always has more than enough food around him. He enjoys eating which explained his growing girth, until he completely and radically changed his diet since returning from LondonO. He has stuck to eating healthily, but maintains that all the stuff he really enjoys is supposedly unhealthy while the healthy stuff often tastes like cardboard or sawdust. He dabbled with a Vegetarian diet for a while before going to LondonO but missed eating meat. Meat seemed more satisfying to his pallet he says. The meat substitutes were passable. Larry says as close as they are supposed to come to a meat taste, it's not the same. He admits he doesn't think it's even close. He ate meat almost every day back in Canada. It was barbeque season after all. That has changed since his return to LondonE. He even has less meat substitutes and only if they are in a mix, like with a stir fry or spaghetti bolognaise (there are a few good mincemeat substitutes actually). He enjoys eating at Vegetarian and Vegan restaurants. They know how to make things taste good and he feels better afterwards. Preparing veggie meals on your own, he says, costs a fortune and is time consuming.

All that aside, let's just say it like it is. Larry loves food no matter how it is served. Most foods anyway. He has a very sweet tooth, like his dad. Larry's dad horded sweets (candies) in his den in LondonO (and everywhere else he had lived) and was reluctant to share them, especially when Larry was around. His dad knew that Larry stole his sweets at every opportunity, so he put out a tin containing the lesser sweets, easy to steal and an acceptable loss. When his dad died in 2010, Larry had the task of cleaning out his dad's den. He found all the very expensive and posh sweets hidden in coat pockets, slippers, a tool box, in a locked drawer of his desk and stashed in two shoe boxes at the top of the room's cupboard. A singularly revelatory moment for Larry. He sensed his dad's disapproval.

BTW (remember that one?) the quote at the beginning of this chapter was not from Confucius. Actually, no one knows who started it. Simply an old proverb. Might have been Larry's mum for all I know. Larry thought it might be funny after the chapter on humour to keep some of you going until the end, a 'wind-up' as they say in Britain. No apologies. Let's move on shall we?

For some reason, Larry thinks food tastes better in England than it does in Canada. Not everyone agrees. Just what he thinks and he's never wrong. Certain foods taste fresher because not as many preservatives are used in food in Europe as they are in North America. Fewer chemicals that are supposed to prevent crop damage are sprayed meaning farmers in Europe seem more aware of improved growing procedures and enhanced land use than overseas (more willing to use green methods anyway). He has watched documentaries verifying this too. It appears that North America is GMO mad (Genetically Modified Organisms) whereas Europe has backed away from the process. Frankenstein tomatoes are not that appealing. Larry buys only organic vegetables and fruits, makes his own granola and now goes mainly to vegetarian restaurants. He juices as much as he eats cooked food. He misses meat when someone fires up a barbeque. But he thinks that, ultimately, his decision is better for him and the planet. He says he feels better too, more energy.

Food is important all over the world and England seems to win the prize for bringing so many different types of it to the table. Larry says he's never seen so many restaurants and take-away (take-out) outlets that serve Indian food. He likens it to the number of donut shops you can find in any town in Ontario, even the villages. The village where he had his first church, with a population under 2,000 has a couple and especially the all-important Tim Hortons, an Ontario institution. In LondonO there are nearly 60 Tim Hortons donut shops and only 4 places that serve Indian food exclusively. Other restaurants serve some Indian food, but specialise in oriental food, pizza and other types of food. In the Borough of Bexley there are more than 50 Indian food outlets and only 1 donut shop listed. Don't ask Larry how the police do without donuts in LondonE. They'll have to make do with poppadoms.

The first Indian restaurant Larry went to was in LondonE. He was 22 years old on his first trip back since his family had moved to Canada. He had never had Indian food before that. They were rare in Ontario in the 1970s. Some of his English cousins took him to a place run by a little Scotsman who had served with the British army as a cook during the late Raj period. The Scottie learned from the best in India and brought the skill back with him to England. Larry's cousins ordered him a chicken phall curry, the hottest dish available. Larry says it's like swallowing lighted gasoline, fire pouring down his throat. They encouraged him to drink water to put the fire out. What they didn't tell him was that water makes it even hotter. Larry gasped, choked, sweated profusely and turned a brilliant shade of red. But he refused to back down and finished the whole meal. By the end, everyone was laughing at the hoodwinked Canadian, even the Scottish chef. Larry was otherwise occupied. He didn't laugh until days later.

Brits are used to the various dishes that came by way of the ships of the Empire bringing every known spice, plant and recipe back to the unloading docks of London in the hay day of British international commerce. A burst of immigration after the Second World War increased the variety of foods making LondonE a culinary haven. When the European Union added further countries from Eastern Europe, many came to Britain and especially LondonE to find work, bringing with them their own delightful recipes. And then there's good old British food, the Sunday roast, Yorkshire puddings, bangers and mash, fish and chips, trifle, treacle tart and spotted dick (to name a few). Larry had to get used to calling some of his favourite vegetables by different names. Egg Plant is an aubergine, zucchinis are courgettes, turnips are swedes and the Brits eat these things called greens. They are a bit like cooked cabbage, but different. Great with gravy and all the other parts of the roast dinner.

The variety is there in Ontario and even LondonO, but fast food is still a staple of many diets. Pizza joints, fast chicken outlets, big chain restaurants that inevitably vie for the steak eaters out there. Ontario is full of them. Barbequed ribs are a big draw and anything pork related. Canadians are big meat eaters. Eating habits have been changing since the turn of the millennium. Larry notices this every time he goes back to Canada. More places serve alternatives to the standard fast food fare. It was a big deal when salads, juices and fruit smoothies were added to hamburger joint menus. Obesity being on the rise with the ensuing heart problems prompted fast food chains to at least appear as if they cared about their customers' health. But when Larry drives the back roads to LondonO from Toronto, through all the small towns, you'll find one long road lined with every fast food franchise imaginable, including, of course, the ubiquitous and obligatory Tim Hortons.

This does not mean that Brits eat a lot healthier. Obesity is a big problem in Britain too. Jamie Oliver, a popular English chef, is forever coming on television to warn Brits about the unhealthy diet they have. He is especially interested in the food served in schools. Children live on chips (French fries), hold the fish, and a sausage called a saveloy. They grab a bag of crisps (potato chips) and drink a cola and eat a chocolate bar or two. That's their meal. One businessman Larry knows is always on the move. His diet is a pork pie, crisps, a cola and a chocolate bar. The choice of a good meal is always there, as it is in Canada, but the fast food bug has come to England in a big way. Most of the familiar North American fast food chains can now be found in LondonE and all over Britain.

When Larry returned for the first time to the land of his birth in 1973, he was already used to the Golden Arches, the colonel's chicken, A&Ws, Harvey's Hamburgers, Red Barn, submarine sandwiches, pizza joints and so on. It shocked Larry to find London so far behind. All they had were Wimpy Burgers (still do), the first American hamburger franchise to enter the UK back in 1955. Larry wishes it were still that way. Britain sold out. The first Wimpy Burger Larry tasted was so bad, he never went back. They really had no idea how to make a proper burger back then. Things certainly have changed. McDonalds came in 1974 to Woolwich, LondonE and the rest followed bit by bit. For the better? No use asking Larry now. Fast food places are anathema to him.

The French eat well and are mostly thin. They were in the 1980s anyway. When Larry went back in 2006 most had stayed pretty thin and the food was as good as ever. Larry is a fan of French cuisine. He made great café au lait and loved the pastries and the general cuisine. The French don't over eat. That's what Larry says. Their portions are always just right and full of healthy ingredients. The French take such pride in their culinary skills that many of the dishes we eat in Canada and England are French inspired. Same with the baked goods and especially the cheeses. The French (it bears repeating) have a different cheese for every day of the year and some left over. Larry loved the food in the south of France the best. He's not a great lover of fish, but there were so many other dishes he loved.

His favourite restaurant in Montpellier was named after something university students use or wear. Larry no longer remembers. The place was a delight. Very inexpensive and the variety of French dishes was staggering. Larry says he drools every time he thinks about it. As a matter of fact, there were so many restaurants on Larry's favourite list and he can't remember one name. They are all very French and quite similar sounding. The memory plays tricks after 25 years plus. He searched the internet for the names and even drove all over Montpellier with Google Street View. So much seems to have changed over time. His favourite places are probably no longer there. But the Golden Arches remain and KFC and some fast food burger joint called Quick still function. Ludicrous.

Wine in France (yes, it's a food....made from grapes) is plentiful and cheap. Larry's years in Marseille were spent searching the local shops for great wines at silly low prices. That was back when the franc was still the French currency. Larry found a little grocery store down the road from him, run by a family of expat Algerians that offered wines from co-op vineyards at prices that even then were ridiculously cheap. For 2.5 francs, which was about $0.25 Canadian at the time, Larry could buy a bottle of Vieux Pape wine (he called it Old Pope). The thing about wines from a co-op is you take what you get. Some small vineyards couldn't produce enough wine on their own to sell on the open market and so banded together. Hit or miss. One bottle of Vieux Pape could taste almost like vinegar, but the next one had a flavour that the best and most expensive wines never could match. For 2.5 francs, the risk was worth it. A good bottle of Vieux Pape, a great brie or camembert and a freshly baked baguette....it's all anyone needs to be happy. Even Marseille looks good afterwards.

The key is to eat well and enjoy it, not eat for the sake of it. Larry's mum is 86 years old now. She tells Larry she has lost her appetite. Nothing tastes good to her any more. Larry has gone on record to say that if that ever happens to him, shoot him. No questions (but leave his mum alone please). If you asked him to pick one of the three countries in which he has lived based on food alone he would choose France. But life is not just about food. There are other things to consider like language and human rights, a willingness to adapt to the surrounding culture, how to earn a living, ease of getting around and, for Larry, what the women are like (the men too but for many different reasons).

And there are always French restaurants in LondonE, even if none of them are in the Borough of Bexley (not exclusively French anyway). LondonO boasts 9 French cuisine restaurants. Not bad. Larry says French cuisine cook books are readily available and classes in all places Canadian and English where you can learn to cook French food. Time to move on to the weather. Larry says he can't tell me any more about his food experiences anyway. He's off to find something to eat.

CHAPTER 11

WEATHER

'Whether the weather is hot or weather the weather cold, whether
the weather is under the weather or whether the weather is not'
(Larry's Mum/Mom)

One thing Larry knows about weather. There're buckets and buckets of it. Everywhere. Violent weather, calm weather, gentle weather, surprising weather and even capricious weather. Larry has seen it all, except for a real tornado, oh, and a full-blown hurricane. But he has seen high winds, very high winds that are the tail end of a hurricane. This past winter in LondonE was the wettest and windiest on record, winds from 80-100 mph. Not a flake of snow all winter, but all the rest. Larry's roof was blown off (well, some of it anyway) and had to be replaced.

Larry wants to see a tornado, from a safe distance that is. He's not sure about a hurricane. Perhaps to experience the full power of one. He's not really sure about that. He has witnessed tornado clouds and extreme heat and cold. Weather patterns have changed in recent years. Larry thinks so. This past winter in LondonE and the one in LondonO have been ridiculously different to former years. Relentless high winds, rains and floods in LondonE and more continuous snow and cold in LondonO than can be remembered. All blamed on some

Arctic Vortex that no one has heard of before, except maybe by some meteorologists who sit in their sunny towers viewing sky maps and their Dopplers all day.

Southern Ontario weather is much affected by the Great Lakes nearly surrounding it, especially in LondonO. Lake effect snow and storms are a big part of LondonO's weather. LondonE is surrounded by the sea, for the most part, and susceptible to the weather crossing over those seas, picking up moisture and dumping it on Britain. Fortunately, the Gulf Stream runs right by the country and brings with it warmer water and air from the Gulf of Mexico. Moderate weather is the result, if not exactly tropical. Milder winters are generally the case.

LondonO is prone to some wild changes in weather. Larry has seen thunder storms that come out of nowhere, raging for a short time then moving off just as quickly. In recent years the threat of tornadoes is ever present. A few have touched down, but most of those are slightly to the east and north through a strange corridor which includes Woodstock to the east of LondonO. Larry drives through a half dozen weather zones in a few short miles around Ontario. Freezing winters are countered by hot, hazy and humid summers. It's really never always that neat and tidy, but you get the idea.

No matter where you're from, weather is the hot (or cold) topic. Folks in LondonO complain just as much about the weather as the good people of LondonE. Larry was in LondonO for the entire spring and summer of 2013. Everyone complained that the spring was too cool and the summer too humid. Meanwhile, back in LondonE, they were having the best summer in years, depending on whom Larry asked when he got back. As the English autumn wore on, some reflected that it was fine for a week or two, but the rest of the summer was 'shit'. The kind of people who always see the glass as half empty. Generally, though, most had no complaints, especially since the previous summers had truly been 'shit'. Larry attests to that. He was there.

LondonE has had its share of crazy weather, especially since Larry returned from Canada to his home in Southeast LondonE. Days of heavy rain, high winds and floods in many areas of England. It was all a part of that Arctic Vortex Larry says, sweeping down from the Arctic, over Canada and across the Atlantic Ocean. In LondonO, it was one of the coldest, snowiest winters on record. Areas of south England and Wales were under water for months. Coastal areas eroded, railway tracks washed away, bridges destroyed and people lost their lives. Weather is a serious business when it goes bad. And it just went bad half way through the summer of 2014 in the south of England. The weather was fine until mid-way through August when Hurricane Bertha decided to leave the east coast of America, travel across the Atlantic and bugger up the English summer.

One thing both sides of the Atlantic have in common is that whenever you meet people, the weather is discussed and no one is ever satisfied with the conditions at the moment of sharing. It's either too hot or too cold, either too humid or too dry and either too much rain or not enough rain. Even when someone admits rain is needed, the person adds, 'But why did it have to come today of all days?' One of Larry's neighbours on his southeast London road, Digger, loves to complain about the weather, no matter the conditions. On one occasion, Larry asked him how he was doing. Digger said he'd be fine if the weather were any better. Larry looked to the sky. It was blue, the sun was out and it was a fairly warm spring day. He said as much to Digger, who replied, "Yeah, but they say there's frost on the weekend." Donald, up the road a bit, is much the same. When the weather turns cold he greets Larry on the street with, "Bloody fucking Canadians, fucking sending us this fucking cold." Larry laughs and walks on by. Donald is mostly harmless.

The topic of weather is an ice-breaker in any culture. "Nice day, isn't it?" can be translated into any language. Complaining about the weather is very English and has spilled over into North America. Ontarians complain about the long, cold winters incessantly. Even in the midst of a record breaking summer heatwave, all an Ontarian can say is, "It's too damned hot, but I'm not going to complain, winter isn't far off….eh." Winter is such a dreaded season that Canadians leave the country in droves, heading anywhere south that's warm. The State of Florida becomes the unofficial 11th Province of Canada from December to March.

Weather in France depends on where you live. It's colder and wetter in the north and drier and sunnier in the south, the best of both climates. Larry witnessed all four seasons during his year in Paris. He saw it all. Paris that springtime was not the most lovable. Lots of rain. He had visitors from Canada and took them to all the usual places, the Eiffel Tower, Montmartre, Notre Dame

Cathedral, Napoleon's tomb in Les Invalides, Versailles and the Louvre. Larry had put together a 20 minute tour of the Louvre, highlighting the main attractions....the Mona Lisa, Venus De Milo, Charlemagne's sword, the Stele of Hammurabi and so on. The day was grey with a constant drizzle rendering outdoor activities soggy. The guests insisted on going to the top of the Arc De Triomphe at the head of Des Champs Elysées.

Gazing down at the traffic below, madly joining the circle of assorted vehicles and just as madly trying to find the spoke of the wheel on which to exit, Larry was joined by a very handsome young man, his incredibly beautiful wife and their three children. None of them had umbrellas. They were soaked from head to foot, but appeared so happy. Larry offered his umbrella to the wife but was refused. The man introduced himself as a Saudi Airline pilot who brought his family to Paris, the city of light, for a holiday. Larry said it was too bad about all the rain. The Saudi man laughed, "Not at all," he said, "This is wonderful. We love the rain. In my country we go out and have a picnic when it rains." To each his own.

In the south of France Larry had to contend with pretty nice weather with the occasional Mistral thrown in for good measure. When that mighty wind blew in, a couple of times a year, things had better be tied down for a few days. Raging down from the Northwest, the winds sweep out into the Mediterranean Sea and have been known to reach 100mph. Many hats are lost by unsuspecting visitors when the Mistral blows. Larry lost one during his first Mistral. Probably being worn by some fisherman now. When the winds are from the deep Sahara to the south, on the other side of the Mediterranean, they bring with them clouds of sand. Everything gets covered in a layer of dust and breathing is difficult. One of those Sand storms was so powerful, it reached England recently. The sky over London went a pinkish yellow. The sand caked the landscape. Larry says you could taste it in the air. He says he refuses to entertain sandwich jokes at this point.

Not much else to say about weather. There's always lots of it and it appears to be getting wackier every year. New meteorological anomalies pop up all the time. Some call it Global Warming, caused to a great extent by people using too many carbon based products. Others say whereas that may be a minor cause, the fact is the world is shifting on its axis and we can expect a polar shift at any time. Still others think everything is fine and we're experiencing temporary phenomena. Religious nuts think we're coming to the end of the world. Larry thinks the world won't end, just the people. He says we've been very arrogant thinking we can control nature and the climate. Now it's biting back.

Larry leaves you with a weather report given by a Cockney presenter (broadcaster). Hat 'n' Feather Forecast: 'Today the Bath Bun will shine over the Borough of Bexley, but there may be some Rawalpindi days next week. In the gypsy's warning there may be some Frarney but no Buck 'n' doe or the dreaded white mice.' See the Epilogue for the translation if you haven't got off your Fife and Drum yet to figure it out.

CHAPTER 12

FLORA & FAUNA

"As custodians of the planet it is our responsibility to deal with all species with kindness, love and compassion." Richard Gere

Except, Mr. Gere, poisonous snakes, crocodiles, mosquitoes, black flies and skunks. The list is much longer. It includes everything that can kill you in Australia, but Larry says we are only dealing with 3 countries….more specifically 2 cities. The picture is clear. Larry says he can respect a rattle snake or a skunk, but he doesn't have to love them. We are getting ahead of ourselves a little. There is less danger in the Flora and Fauna of LondonO and LondonE than in one city block of anywhere in Australia. Some of the Flora and Fauna in those two cities are more of a nuisance than dangerous. A look at both will demonstrate this.

One thing Larry knows about Flora and Fauna, other than what they mean, is the variety of both and how they overwhelms him. The types and names of plants and flowers he has had in various gardens through the years mystify him. The differences between Hydrangea and Wisteria, Clematis and Bougainvillea and Fuchsia and any other flowering plant make Larry's head spin. He has one or two of them in his garden but he's never sure which ones, let alone trying to pronounce their names.

One other thing Larry does know is weeds. He always, like everyone, has plenty of them. Even weeds seem to vary according to climate and the country in which they are found. Larry remembers thistles in Canada and some clover looking weed, crab grass, dandelions and one that has what looks slightly like a marijuana leaf (no, he's checked), but there are too many to name. He doesn't know what they are anyway. He went online to check the types of weeds that grow in Ontario. Unbelievable. They were alphabetised. Larry says he stopped counting after the L's (for Larry) and had reached 119 species including, under the 'L' Lady's Thumb and Purple Loostrife, the latter being a scourge in Ontario for years from the early 1990s. Purple Loostrife came from Europe aboard ships that used soil, containing Loostrife seeds, for the ballast in the 19th century. A beautiful purple flower arranged in towers make the weed intoxicatingly desirable, but the roots system can choke the life out of marsh areas, wiping out indigenous plant species.

Larry wonders why weeds are so prolific and grow anywhere without invitation while garden flowers and plants are incredibly delicate and fragile, requiring tender care and constant attention in order to maintain them. Don't worry, he knows the answer to that question, but doesn't like it. Survival of the fittest and all that. Same kind of question as why tasty food is bad for us but bland, mushy goo is good for us. Back to weeds. Larry says he got a kick out of the name Hairy Nightshade. Then he discovers its berries are extremely toxic to humans and other animals while the plant itself harbours spores that can kill crops and wreak havoc on orchard fruits and low lying berries. Nasty stuff….unless you happen to be a Hairy Nightshade.

Weeds are much the same everywhere now thanks to international travel. Weeds adapt easily almost anywhere. Many of them are very attractive looking which makes it impossible to hate them and more difficult to want to eradicate them. Some people even grow Purple Loostrife in their gardens. 'Idiots', says Larry. In LondonE, Larry battles thistles (and curses the Scots while doing so), bind weed that wraps itself around everything and stinging nettles. The stingers seem to jump at Larry's hand when he gets anywhere near them. Thankfully, Dock Leaf is nearby to rub away the sting. He learned that trick from his best friend. The rest of Larry's weeds are the typical garden variety, remaining unnamed and unwanted. Lazy Larry wants to astro turf his garden and have those very realistic plastic plants and flowers adorn the space. Thankfully he has no money to do it. Instead, nature takes its course….as it ought.

Larry lives in the County of Kent known as the Garden of England. He loves the carpets of Bluebells in the wooded areas of the county. The southeast of England is a regular Eden. Not that Larry believes an Eden ever existed, but Kent comes close to the myth. One thing Larry noticed when he arrived in England, and his home in Bexley was the variety of roses growing everywhere, even in the front lots of many of the homes in Bexleyheath and Welling. The old timers tend to feature them. Younger people or those from elsewhere pave over the front gardens for their cars. Larry loves the rose bushes. So many colours and the fragrance is lovely. Nothing beats the English red rose. It is, after all, the national flower. France's national flower is the Iris (another woman's name) and for Canada it's the….not a flower but a leaf, the Maple Leaf as the Maple tree is the national tree and a beaver that cuts maples down (not the preference, but it happens) with its teeth is the national animal. The European beaver was hunted to extinction in Britain, like the lynx, wolf and other species.

Ontario has the trillium as its provincial flower. Larry saw thousands of them during his walks through the Medway Valley Heritage Forest in LondonO. The place was full of Flora, left to its own devices with decaying trees, fallen trees, new growth and all kinds of other wild plants and flowers. Picking a trillium can bring a fine or even jail time. They ought to have a law for trees like that. On one of Larry's morning walks, he skirted the upper ridge above a tributary of LondonO's River Thames (you heard it right), nature on one side and big houses on the other. As he passed one of the homes, he encountered a torrent of water pouring across the foot path, down the cliff and into the river. He wondered where the source was and looking up to the home in question saw some stupid homeowner draining his swimming pool over his lawn and into the Heritage Forest. Bad water (chlorinated) and erosion. Larry reported it later to the conservation authority who said they would deal with the issue. He hopes they did.

People generally take care of their gardens in LondonO. The trend these days is to buy some of those large, flat rocks from the Canadian Shield or the Muskoka area of Ontario….cottage country. The rocks are worked into the lawn with planted shrubs and flowers all around them, making it seem like the house is in cottage country. Very effective. Presents a slight problem for reselling if it isn't the taste of those buying the house, but Larry says the new owners could cover up the rocks and have a little hill to roll down or put a statue on top or pay lots of money to have the rocks removed. When they are put in front and back, the effect is one of a fortress, impregnable and safe. Lots of people just have a regular garden at the back, a few border flowers in front and a big lawn to mow. Ah, the suburbs. LondonO has done well to preserve a lot of green space despite all the box store areas. But then, when you're in the middle of nowhere, surrounded by so much land, green spaces aren't hard to find.

Parks in LondonE are just that, parks. Pro or anti-Royalist, everyone has to at least thank the Royals for the huge swaths of parkland in and around LondonE. The other Lords and Ladies gave their lands for parks as well. Not that they gave the land up easily or willingly, but the public is thankful. Such great areas of green with ready-made gardens, sculpted trees and manicured lawns. I've told you about Larry's love of Danson Park near his home. An old mansion house sits in the middle of the park surrounded by fields rolling down to a lake.

Across from the mansion grows an old English country garden that has changed considerably since Larry moved to the area. Once full of flowers, it has become an overgrown country garden with various grasses and reed beds featured. The trees in the park are many and varied, though storms packing high winds have taken their toll. People walk their dogs, boaters are on the lake, fishermen and women fish from the banks of the lake, secret paths lead into deep wooded areas and a very large oak tree sits, guarded by a fence and all alone, in the middle of the huge front lawn (big enough for about 12 football pitches). The old horse stables are now a restaurant that changes management every 5 minutes. Always a festival going on there now, the latest being fireworks for Guy Fawkes Night. Brilliant place.

Larry loves Greenwich Park and Regents Park in LondonE. In fact, he hasn't visited a park in the city or around it that hasn't impressed him. Money can do that. It shapes a park into a kind of magical place. Larry says you're in the city but not of it when wandering around one of the parks in LondonE. And he hasn't seen them all yet. The parks in France are much the same and also from Royalty, except they were taken this time, from the king and his nobles. The parks of Paris are a wonder, even if one was taken over by the Disney people and turned into one of their theme parks. The grounds of Versailles are magnificent and have been preserved as they were in the days of the monarchy for posterity. The Parc de Sceaux, down the road from where Larry lived in Paris, is a mini Versailles and the home of Colbert who wanted his place to resemble the grounds around Versailles. In Marseille Larry lived among palm trees, the first he'd seen in a natural environment. Larry loves trees. Hugs them regularly....in his mind. He's not that crazy....yet.

Gardening has never been Larry's strength. He hasn't the patience for it. In England, people in the cities have access to something called allotments. Entire swaths of land are put aside and divided into 50 to 400 metre lots. A lottery exists giving people the chance to win an allotment when one becomes available (rarely). Larry walks by a local one quite often and sees some old-timers hoeing or weeding, tending their non-commercial piece of land, growing vegetables and a few fruits. Larry likes the idea of growing his own fresh vegetables, but the grocery shop (store) is so close and he doesn't want to put anyone out of work because he no longer needs their produce.

If the Flora of any of the three countries is rather similar, including the weeds, the Fauna couldn't be more different. Any of the large predatory animals that once existed in England were hunted into extinction long ago, including bears. Strange that the national animal for England is the Barbary Lion when there isn't a lion to be seen, except in the zoos and don't get Larry going on about those. The symbol probably comes from that used by medieval warriors. King Richard the Lionhearted comes to mind, he of the Crusades. Strange how symbols come about and remain.

The biggest predator in LondonE is the fox. Driven from the countryside by aggressive fox hunts sponsored by the privileged class, the fox has taken up residence in the back gardens, under old sheds and anywhere they can burrow in the city. They are mostly an unwelcomed guest, but so far, except for a few random attacks on humans, they have coexisted with the dominant species. They trash the trash, shit everywhere and have an annoying bark when mating. Larry thinks he has one, or two, living under his music studio. He hopes they like Joe Bonamassa.

Other than that, there are bunny rabbits and grey squirrels, red squirrels, hedgehogs (cute little things), mice of all sorts, voles, shrew, a polecat or two, even less wild boar, weasels, the ubiquitous rat, cats (lots of cats), dogs (lots of them too) and guinea pigs. Brits love them. Just outside of London are found deer (larger than foxes but not dangerous….usually) and the real toughy, the Badger. Larry hasn't seen one yet. Doesn't want to either. They can be testy, like wolverines in Canada. They'll avoid us, but don't go onto their territory. The dog is king of the land here. As in France. Over there they have more laws protecting dogs than humans. In LondonE, dogs are part of nearly every household. Larry's too busy to have one, or be had by one. But with dogs comes the inevitable pavement (sidewalk/trottoir) poo. Some scoop. Canadians are better at it than Brits. In Bexley, the pavements have painted stencils of a dog sitting over his poo with the words, 'clean it up' under the poo. They have faded and some have disappeared. Dogs can't read anyway and dog owners either do or don't scoop and no diagram is going to change that. Just makes it look like politicians are doing something. Right.

Ontario is another thing entirely. Bear, wolves, coyotes, wildcats, lynx (a wildcat), raccoons, skunks, porcupines, deer, elk, moose, possums, fishers (that don't eat fish), woodchucks, groundhogs, chipmunks and squirrels (grey, black and red). Don't ask Larry about red squirrels. They are his mortal enemy. LondonO, being in the middle of nowhere, has many of these species. You won't see bears, wolves or moose there, but foxes and even coyotes are about. Deer are everywhere. The pests of the bunch are the skunks and raccoons. Every village, town and city is plagued with them. Larry encountered skunks on his walks around London. Fine if you see them from a distance and have time to avoid them, but deadly if surprised. Not lethal, just deadly. The spray they let go is so toxic, it can burn the eyes and linger for days if you happen to get sprayed.

Larry once opened the back door of his house in Tweed, Ontario to find a skunk sitting on the porch. Both species were surprised. Larry closed the door instantly, just as the skunk released its spray, hitting the door. But the fumes penetrated the entire house. Larry was choking and his eyes burned. He herded the family into the basement of the house and waited for the smell to dissipate. For days afterwards, all you could smell was skunk. They are cute little things, but not to be trifled with.

Raccoons are just annoying. They wear the bandit mask over their eyes well. They get into everything and generally take what they like. Their paws, more like hands, can open jars. They can walk tight ropes and get into the smallest openings. One place Larry lived in while in seminary was a mansion formerly owned by the Weston family. In Canada they own the largest food processing and distribution company under George Weston Limited. They bequeathed the house and properties to the Presbyterian Church to be used as a home for unwed mothers.

An apartment complex (really a dormitory) was built onto the mansion. The grounds are substantial. The wealthy live in this part of Clarkson, Ontario. Larry was just housesitting as the church needed someone on the premises for security. His family stayed in Tweed where Larry was the student minister at the time. Larry went back on weekends but rattled around the big mansion all week, all by himself. A large mural had been painted in the downstairs hallway along the walls. The scene was of County Armagh in Ireland, the old Weston family home county. The painter was one of the family sent from Ireland to live with the Canadian relatives to have a baby 'out of wedlock' as they put it in days of yore. Meant to avoid scandal and explains the later use for the property. The young woman spent her 9 months painting the mural, complete with a castle.

Larry's bedroom upstairs was enormous as were all the rooms. The old place creaked and groaned in the still of the night. Larry often wondered if a ghost or two were hanging about. He began to hear strange scratching noises that seemed to emanate from the floor in his room. Every time he went to investigate, the scratching stopped. This went on for months. Then one night he was awoken sharply by a piercing screech followed by what sounded like two animals fighting. More screeching. The sounds came from under the floor in his bedroom. Larry banged on the floor with the end of his baseball bat (kept by the side of his bed in case he had the sudden urge to hit a home run). To no avail. This went on for several more nights. Turns out two raccoons were living under his floor. How they got there was anyone's guess. Mating season apparently.

Larry got the animal protection people in to trap and remove the couple to a more suitable location (for Larry). All became quiet again until one night, months later, Larry heard something on the lower roof outside his bedroom window. There, in the moonlight, walking as stealthily as possible, waddled a mother raccoon and four babies. They stopped, looked right at Larry and the mother seemed to smile and say, "Thought you could get rid of us eh? Well.... we're back." Uncanny creatures.

I've told you Larry's bear story already. He's had no such encounters in England. Well, that's not quite true. The fiercest attack on his person has been from spiders and their webs. Larry's garden is crawling with spiders of a wide range. Most are not harmful, but the big ones can deliver a nasty bite. They spin their webs everywhere, between everything and wait for their prey. They're not expecting Larry, but I'm sure he'd do in a pinch. You've never seen anyone lose it so completely until you've seen Larry run into one of those webs, inadvertently pulling the spider onto his person and suddenly turning into a frenzied dancer. It has happened more than once. The dance continues.

The only encounter in France was a near miss with a scorpion on the wall of his flat in Montpellier. But it wasn't a deadly one. Still, the sting would have hurt. The creature looked menacing enough. Other than that, Fauna was never a large part of Larry's years in France. He managed to avoid Fauna for some reason. He saw lots of dogs. As he said, dogs rule in France. Mostly they are the small ones. He has seen dogs carried as much as walked. The French don't have children, so they spoil their dogs. Why not.

Snakes are no problem for Larry. He stays well clear. Not seen any yet in England. He once had a Massasauga rattle snake slither over his hiking boots in Cyprus Lake Provincial Park north of LondonO, but neither party wanted to stay around to find out who was toughest. Larry doesn't like the feel of snakes and hasn't handled one. He is generally afraid of Fauna. Doesn't know why really. Dogs bit him when he was young on his way home from school. But he loves dogs. You can keep cats. Never been on a horse. Not interested. The Hitchcock movie 'The Birds' made Larry suspicious of the flying Fauna, especially if he sees them in bunches.

A seagull once stole Larry's sandwich right out of his hand while he was endeavouring to eat it, sitting peacefully on his beach chair at Sauble Beach, northwest of LondonO. In LondonE, someone released (by mistake) two small parakeets (south American munks apparently) and now there are thousands of the green things squawking their way around parks and residential areas. They are actually noisier than crows. The real terror of the skies around Larry's place in Welling are the Magpies, those beautifully blue/black/white feathered nuisances that are the noisiest of all birds and drive out the song birds, issuing a cackle that grates on the nerves. A gang of them decided to take over the trees around Larry's place. All the lovely song birds can be heard further up the road, waiting for the interlopers to move on before returning to serenade Larry once again. We shall not discuss Canada geese and their invasion of LondonE. Bullies. Worse than Magpies.

And that's all Larry has to say about nature. He loves it all....in its place and outside his house. Beware all spiders and other insects that try to get in his house to get out of the cold. I think that we've established that Larry doesn't believe there's a God in a place called heaven. His prerogative. But he puts an addendum on that. If there just happened to be one, or more or some super creator of some sort he has one question: What the hell were you thinking when you made mosquitoes?!?

CHAPTER 13

CHARACTERS

"A man's true character comes out when he's drunk." Charlie
Chaplin

Two things Larry knows about people. First, there are a lot of them everywhere, except for maybe in deserts, under the seas and on the top of high mountains (although Mount Everest is over-populated these days). Second, most of them are characters, on both sides of the ocean. The Atlantic may be a great divide in terms of customs and culture, but characters abound on both sides. France wins the character department, England, not to mention Scotland, Wales and Northern Ireland, are not far behind in Larry's estimation. Canada, and in particular, Ontario, have their share of oddballs, another word for characters, but Larry isn't quite as objective when it comes to them. He was raised there and, being quite odd himself, sees other odd Ontarians as normal.

I suppose the definition of a character, other than being an oddball, might be an eccentric. You can find that in the Oxford dictionary. I'm not talking about people with character…. strong, determined, courageous people, for example. Some characters can be those things, but usually characters live for themselves and are notable for their foibles rather than anything noble. That certainly is the case of the people living on streets where Larry has lived. This is not to say that the characters in question are bad people. On the contrary, some of them are fine folk. Quirky perhaps, a little lost in worlds of their own making maybe, hiding many secrets with umpteen skeletons in all closets for sure. But then who hasn't? These are the people that have been brought into Larry's life, for better or worse, richer or poorer, certifiably crazy or coolly rational. Larry, by the way, is all of them too.

Oddballs come in every shape and size and may appear normal to most people, but upon closer inspection display tendencies toward irrational and bizarre behaviours....at least according to Larry. They say it takes one to know one. We've covered that ground. On the street on which Larry lives in southeast London, a microcosm of humanity lives. There's Digger (not his real name surely) a few doors down and the guy across the street who is an Elvis Presley nut (call him Elvis, Larry does), Donald the octogenarian womaniser, Jim the roofing man and Jim the other roofing man, a paramedic (one of the roofing Jim's wife), a woman who does in-house spray tans, her husband who has never stopped improving their house, a couple of Pikeys (Gypsies or Travellers.... who don't really travel), Sax (not his real name but close) and his wife, Gus (Brazillian/Potuguese/Italian) and his Latvian family, a mysterious Nigerian family at the end of the road with big black SUVs, a couple across the street who had a baby no one knew about and a host of people down the end of the street never met and not known, except for the noise they make occasionally when late night fights or impromptu parties break out.

There have been others. The house across the street from Larry had the family from hell for the first couple of years of Larry's life on the street. The dad was always at a local betting office. The mum could be heard screaming a mile away at three boys, well, monsters really. The eldest looked like Shrek....honestly. They loved to provoke the neighbours by kicking their football against our cars and homes. Larry had to go out several times to have a word. They would run into the safety of the house, emerging when the all clear was sounded by their mum. One time one of the neighbours went over to have a word with the mum. She just hid inside and could be heard muttering that she wasn't going to deal with all that right now. She never did. After the fourth baby arrived, a girl, the family mercifully moved. No tears were shed.

The next occupants, if you can call them that, were a gang of Pikeys (Gypseys/Travellers) who, over the course of their stay, tore out every piece of pipe, the boiler and the wiring in the place to sell as scrap. The main chap was as lugubrious as he was cunning, a weasel if ever there was one in human form. He sweet-talked the neighbours and scared us all at the same time. These people will do anything to get their way. One time a group of them showed up at a local golf course and paved the parking lot without having a work permit or the owner's knowledge of any transaction between them. When the owner challenged them, they said if he didn't pay up they would do him a mischief (not a good thing). He paid.

One day the chief Pikey brought a big dog to the place across the street. A mean, surly looking thing. And the lights were left on day and night. No one asked. The authorities came by a couple of times to check the premises, but a thick sheet was strategically placed over the front window to hide the nefarious goings on inside. Turns out they were growing marijuana. Surprise. But the powers-that-be are strapped by laws that protect even the worst offenders and can only knock on the door to ask politely if all is well inside, hoping to catch a glimpse of what may truly be taking place. Rarely occurs. A new task force like the FBI in America has recently been formed in Britain, but the case load is such that many wrongdoers slip through the cracks, especially Pikeys.

So one day the dog escapes, jumps out of the top window and somehow survives to terrorise the neighbourhood. Pikey number one comes home to find the dog has gone and runs across to Larry's place to ask if he's seen his dog. Larry says no. The man genuinely looks distraught. Could he actually have real feelings or is he worried about the damage the dog could be doing, alerting the law and bringing judgement day down on his head? Somehow he finds the dog and within a couple of days, the place is cleared out. The Pikeys are gone. The house has been gutted and the absent landlord will have to pay for the damages. But the Pikeys were no paying tenants, just squatters. The landlord was some ailing old guy who lived far away and never visited his property. Only Elvis next door watched the house for him, being extremely careful not to piss off the Pikeys in case of reprisals. When the Pikeys had finally left the building, Elvis put a locking gate leading to the back, cut the grass in the back garden and tidied up the front. No one has lived there since.

For a long time, Larry saw unmarked police cars and police vans down the road on countless mornings either staking out or entering a home, confiscating cars and harassing the tenant(s). Some nasty piece of work lived there. So nasty he beat his own mother up on several occasions. The friends he had over were not the savoury type either. One morning a paddy wagon, two unmarked cars and three police cars arrived. After that, all was quiet. Larry's not sure what went down, but peace was restored. The same happened on Larry's side of the street too. Peace that is. But of a different variety.

When Larry moved into his place, no one lived in the house attached to his. For several years this was the case. But the house next to that contained a very nice lady with mad daughters. One in particular Larry liked to call Gobby. She had a mouth on her that turned the air on Larry's street bluer than an episode of Californication. She yelled at her poor mum and anyone else who got in her way....morning, noon and night (especially night). She screamed inside the house loud enough for all to hear and then outside on the street. She yelled at the police when they were called because of the ruckus and the ambulance drivers who would come to take her away. When she came back she started screaming all over again. Crazy as a loon. They all finally moved away. Now Sax and his wife live there....quiet as church mice. Passing Larry on the street, Sax just nods. Never a word between them.

A few doors down from there lived (past tense thankfully) a family of few scruples and even worse morals. Larry doesn't like to judge. Everybody says that of course, but Larry finds himself judging anyway in cases that affect him directly and detrimentally. When his peace is broken, he judges. Enough said. The woman of the house was rough, rude and rancorous. She could be seen walking along the pavement, in her PJs with a glass of wine in her hands calling on a neighbour or two to imbibe along with her. Sometimes she'd just yell at her kids as she wandered along the pavement drinking her wine. One of her sons was a lovely young man. Larry hopes he stays that way. The odds are against him, but there is hope. The youngest, Frankie was the opposite. A little shit disturber if ever there was one. He led his siblings up and down the street, banging on doors, ringing door bells and running away, running his bicycle into parked cars (on purpose), inciting little Charlie (Chaz they called him) next door to throw things into Larry's garden and every so often, when Larry was out, climbing into the garden over the fence to snoop around.

One afternoon Larry saw Frankie with Chaz in the garden next door plotting something. Larry watched them from his bedroom window upstairs. They were about to lob things into Larry's garden when he yelled from behind a curtain that if they dared, they would both die instantly (don't judge). The two scallywags had no idea where the voice was coming from. They looked all around and then beat a hasty retreat into Chaz's house. Frankie's family also moved soon after that. So did Chaz's. Larry takes no credit for it. Neither does he want to get into a debate about people living in council housing. Things almost calmed down until the new folk moved in next door. They have two children who don't stop crying. Most of the time it's more attention seeking than anything real. When they are in the garden they scream. Constant noise. Larry doesn't claim to be the perfect parent, but these kids were never in bed before 11pm and were up crying around 5am. The only peace Larry gets is when the mother takes her children back to Latvia to the family farm for long stretches at a time. Never long enough for Larry.

The family living beside Elvis moved before Larry returned from LondonO the last time he was there. Larry taught their young, very high strung child guitar lessons. Nice kid, but a mess whenever his extremely overbearing, feisty Brazilian mum attended lessons. Larry preferred the dad. He's English, from Sheffield, calm and easy going. Mum was a nightmare. The poor kid dissolved into tears when his mum was there. She pushed him and cajoled him mercilessly if he didn't perform to her standards of perfection. Poor kid. Larry felt sorry for the dad too. He would have asked the mum to stay away, but he has a policy not to be with young children alone. You never know these days. Have to be careful. They can't be trusted.

Then there's Larry. But we know enough about him to write a book. Let's talk about Donald for a moment, the prize character of the street. Donald is one of those Englishmen who knows everything about everything. He has an opinion on every subject and, naturally, his opinion is correct. He goes for long walks every day, poking his nose into everyone's business without a by-your-leave. If someone (anyone) is in front of his or especially her house, Donald will stop and either give his opinion on something about the person or their house or he'll jump into an ongoing discussion. Larry says Donald's eye for the ladies is more than noticeable. For a man in his seventies, Donald acts like a teenager in front of women. His silent wife, Larry has only seen her a few times over the years he's lived on the street, must have to put up with a lot.

Donald walks everywhere. He likes to tell you about his days in the army, post war army that is. And he loves to make fun of Larry being a Canadian. It's all banter, but Donald takes it to another level. Everything he says to Larry has to end with, "but what the fuck would a fucking Canadian fucking know about that?" He is singularly wearing out the word fuck. But only when he talks to males. To the ladies he is syrupy smooth, almost to the point of silliness. So transparent is Donald that the women hide if they are lucky enough to see him coming. Often he sneaks up on his prey catching them unaware. Then the one-way flirting begins. If there are workers about he'll stop and banter. If he sees the back gate open and someone working in their garden or workers toiling on the garden, he'll walk in uninvited to see what's going on. He has no qualms about any of it.

One time, Larry decided if you can't beat them....you know the rest. He was effing his way through some controversial topic involving the Tories and the Labour Party when Donald stopped Larry and said, "'Ere, you fucking should fucking watch your fucking language mate. There might fucking be some fucking ladies about." Larry says he would have laughed if Donald hadn't been so dead serious. Now Larry tries, like the ladies, to avoid Donald as best he can. But the other morning Larry was walking home from the grocery store and couldn't avoid Donald as he approached his house. Donald hailed Larry with the usual, "What the fuck is fucking wrong with fucking Canada, fucking sending us all this fucking cold fucking weather in fucking August. Fucking Wankers." Larry wanted to say....well you can guess. Instead he smiled and said, "It's paying the Brits back for Marmite." Donald just grunted and carried on past, probably looking for some lady to chat up.

Larry has lived on many streets in Canada over the years, all with characters but nothing like the present road. When Larry was young he lived in a town called Whitby in Ontario. One of the neighbour girls used to defecate on Larry's doorstep if she was upset with Larry or his brother. In another town, the family across the street were all stark raving mad. They put clothes on backwards sometimes to be different and boasted they had the first colour TV in all Aurora. This was in 1957. It was actually a piece of glass tinted in blue at the top, green in the middle and red and yellow on the bottom placed in front of the TV screen.

As an adult, Larry lived on streets in Canada with all types of characters, but again never as colourful as the ones on his present street. The oddest Canadian neighbours lived on streets in towns removed from the Toronto influence. In a village where Larry lived, the neighbours were typical village people....countrified, living at a slower pace than city folk. Larry had officiated the wedding of the couple next door. They were true potheads and loved to party. At about 3am in the morning, one particular party was still rolling along when Larry decided he had to say something. In a few hours he'd be preaching and needed some sleep. Just as he got up to yell out the window, a new country song came on their stereo, 'Achy Breaky Heart' by Billy Ray Cyrus. Very catchy. Larry decided to go with it. To this day, every time he hears that song he thinks of Cal and Lorraine. They've broken up since (Larry's track record for marriages he's performed remaining together is not good) but memories live forever. Larry did have a word with Cal the next day. Cal apologised profusely. But the next party went just as late, country music blaring, pot and liquor induced laughter and Cal yelling up to Larry's window, "Sorry Rev, we'll be done soon." Never happened. Larry learned how to fall asleep with the racket.

The couple on the other side of Larry were much older and had lived in the village all their lives. They moved slowly and talked slowly. Like living next door to turtles. But Keith had such wit. You had to wait for it but it would eventually spill out. Down the road lived an extremely odd character whose singular mission in life was to remind the village of its heritage. Every penny he had and every penny some others had and were cajoled to part with went into buying an old house and then building a large, fireproof side building to house the thousands of old artifacts this character begged, borrowed and otherwise pried from the hands of, at least, the living. He found unusual ways to donate his own money to his own cause just to get the tax break. When locals died, this chap went to the funerals, making donations to his own place (remember that one?) even if the family requested they go to a charity they deemed important such as cancer research or some heart foundation. Didn't matter if people laughed at him, he ploughed on.

One fine afternoon this character was walking by Keith's place and noticed some railroad ties Keith had used to border his front lawn and garden. He knocked on Keith's door and said that he had seen these ties and wondered if Keith would care to donate them to his museum. He was putting together a railroad exhibit. Keith pointed out that the ties were brand new, not antique at all. Our character was undeterred. He said, "Yes, but Keith, in 40 years they'll be much older." Keith looked at him like he was in the presence of some escapee from the nut house and told him to go away, but in stronger terms.

A few doors down lived Dick. A man's man. He was a member of every service club going…. Lions, Rotary, Masonic Lodge, the lot. And he golfed all the time. Larry had never played golf until he came to this village. A member of his congregation had a stroke and one day when Larry visited him in his home, he announced that he was giving his set of golf clubs to Larry because the good reverend needed to relax. Yeah, right. Anyway, another member of the congregation took it upon himself to teach Larry how to play the game. He was a patient man. During the first lesson, on the first hole, Larry flailed away at the ball, missing more than hitting it when Dick happened to drive by. He stopped his car, got out and proceeded, with folded arms over his ample belly, to watch Larry struggle. After about ten minutes without Larry making much progress, Dick yelled, "Hey, Rev. Stick to tennis!"

Apart from Larry's street, there were plenty of characters in the rest of the village. There's Norm Bolger a welfare ne're-do-well. He couldn't work because he was too shy. But never too shy to start fights. The welfare cheque was spent on cases of beer and a bicycle he rode around the village all day long wearing a number 27 Toronto Maple Leafs jersey (Frank Mahovlich and Darryl Sittler would not have been proud). He'd finish one tour of the village, passing by Larry's house, then begin again. At night he could be found in the local watering hole singing karaoke after consuming a few. Maybe he ought to have worked in a beer store, inebriated. Another character used to come up with crazy ideas every five minutes and try to give them away to turn them into something concrete. These were no inventions, just ideas and philosophical wanderings. Bob would sit with his buddies and scatter ideas like a machine gun until someone either told him to shut up or sit somewhere else. It's too bad really. Bob was like a fish-out-of-water in this rather staid village. Norm and Bob might have thought about getting together and starting up an enterprise. An intelligently run courier service perhaps.

Characters surfaced all throughout Larry's life in Canada. The bosses he worked for were all characters. Mr. Steiger, the son of a Nazi SS officer who ran a grocery store with an iron fist. And he always wore a brown shirt. Larry wondered. Another German boss, this time Jewish, had the most pompous way of behaving in front of both his staff and customers. He stood in front of those gathered about him and posed much like Mussolini, hands turned outwards on hips and head raised in the air. Then he made announcements about something totally irrelevant to the situation, wheeled and turned, walking back to his office. Larry worked for two more Jewish bosses. Not that their ethnicity is important except that the ones Larry worked for had this way of acting as if they were in possession of something anyone not of their kind had no way of obtaining.

Ted Goldman wanted to be in a partnership with Larry. Ted spirited Larry away from Mussolini to work for him in Vancouver, British Columbia. Ted was an intense, wide-eyed guy, always hustling, speaking quickly to save time for business. He told Larry he wanted to leave the business in 5 years to live on a kibbutz in Israel. The boss was on a trip to California one time when a couple of Vancouver police detectives came into the showroom and asked Larry what it was like to work for a wife killer. Larry knew the story about a man Ted hired to do some odd jobs who broke in to Ted's place one night when he was away and murdered his wife. The killer told the cops Ted had hired him to do the deed. It was never proven. Who knows? Anyway, it unsettled Larry, especially when they kept coming in to question him. What did he know? When Larry told Ted what had happened, Ted just shrugged, like it was not news and he was used to police harassment. Lovely. Larry left the business soon after. He has always wondered if Ted ever made it to his kibbutz.

Mr. Sobol was in the steel business, a man with a large girth and a perpetually red face, sitting behind his desk wearing his diamond encrusted rings (one for each finger) passing down orders to the plebes who did his bidding. For some reason he took a shine to Larry. That's because Larry consulted Mr. Sobol before every sale. Those sales guys who didn't were not long for the company. The pay was lousy, but Larry stayed because he was soon going to be leaving for France. Now there's a land of characters to be sure. Larry says he has never met a French person who isn't odd, but odd in a different way to the rest of Larry's kind. His boss in France was a strange man, but English. The overall boss was a Canadian, not weird but exacting, very uptight. Mennonite. Reminded Larry of his old football (not soccer) coach.

The French characters Larry met were from a variety of ethnic backgrounds. The walls of Larry's apartment on Avenue De La Rose in Marseille were paper thin. A very loud, very orthadox Tunisian Jewish family lived next door to Larry. The man of the house made his own medicinal concoctions for god knows what and wanted to use Larry as a guinea pig. Larry tried one just to be polite. That was the last one. The neighbour had a cure for everything. They were the unhealthiest family on earth. The kids, all ten of them in a three bedroom apartment, seemed to be ill all the time. The wife said 'hoy' a lot and Larry put up with the noise.

The French don't really like anyone who isn't French. Somehow the rest of the world lacks the true intellect that only the French possess. Everything is a putdown, worse than the English, but then they are cousins of a sort, whether they acknowledge it or not. And both have contempt for one another. Perfect match. As for the rest of the French characters Larry met, the most prominent are those from officialdom, the immigration officers, police, post office workers, shop keepers (especially in Paris) and train conductors. Their contempt for non-French people knew no bounds.

Larry stopped at a roadside café just outside Grenoble with some friends (American, Canadian and British) one summer for some ice cream. They sat at a table outdoors under an umbrella advertising Kronenbourg 64 beer. The sun was shining and all was right with the world. A rather dapper man came out and asked those assembled what they'd like. They inquired as to the kinds of ice cream he had. He pointed out, oh so politely with only a hint of irritation, that had they bothered to come inside his establishment, they would have seen the list of available items. He went over the entire inventory methodically and with a hint of pride in his demeanor. Then the American asked him how much they were. The man said he would be back in a moment, turned and went inside his shop.

An inordinate amount of time passed before a young girl came out and asked those assembled what they would like to order. Slightly bemused by this turn of events, the group asked what had happened to the man who had been serving them. She replied, ever so sweetly, "My father says you send children to deal with children." The Canadians, the American and the two Brits got up, without ordering anything, and drove away, angry, but somewhat chastened. Not much else can be said about the French. Larry met some good ones, but these tended to be citizens who were more cosmopolitan in their outlook, forsaking their own French code of superiority to join the rest of us who struggle through life doing the best we can with what we've got wherever we're from.

Larry wanted me to tell you about some of the characters he's met while teaching guitar lessons in LondonE. But before we get to the students, Larry says the boss he worked for in LondonE (and where his original guitar students came from) was one of the oddest people he has ever met. Nigel Plimp (certainly not his real name) opened a music shop in one of Europe's largest indoor malls, located inside an old chalk quarry. Larry was fortunate enough to get a job there when he first moved to LondonE. He told a few porkies (you non Brits remember that one) to get the spot. As his resumé coach told him, "Bull-shit baffles brains." The boss saw himself as a self-made entrepreneur who was going to take over the world. He actually said it and meant it.

Nigel radiated the air of a pompous Frenchman, but the characteristics of an Englishman out of his depth and into a maelstrom of indecision. He liked to think he was in charge and acted accordingly, but he hadn't a clue what to do. That, and he was more interested in show than substance. Nigel was the consummate image guy. He ought to have been a hairdresser. He drove his staff mad with orders that made no sense, meant to assert his control when none was needed. The man was all about the money. He had to feed his appetite for fine cars and beautiful women, even though he was married.

When Larry began his stint at the shop, the staff members were told that Nigel had his own guitar making factory in China. He gave his guitars hip names,

'Jasper-Portus' for the acoustics and 'Sabre' for the electrics. He even beat up one of the electrics and sold it for a fortune because he said it now looked vintage. The problem was, the guitars in question were rubbish by most standards, but sold for much cheaper prices to woo the uninitiated. Despite the brand names, it was obvious to the staff that these guitars were mass produced in a Chinese factory making generic guitars for thousands of shops around the world. Larry found fool proof evidence of this while unpacking a black lacquered 'Jasper-Portus' one time. Underneath the 'Jasper Portus' name on the headstock of the guitar could be seen very faintly the name 'Kreuger'. Someone in Woo Hoo Province, China, had made a mistake and did his (or her) best to cover it up. Not good enough. Larry took the guitar to Nigel and pointed out the faux pas. Undeterred and unmoved he said, "That just makes it even cooler. Add £20 to the price." The audacity of a silly man.

But the clincher for character-of-that-year award goes to Nigel for wearing a fluorescent green guitar patch cord (cable) around his head like a sweat band, a pink fluorescent cable around one arm and a purple one around the other, an Iron Maiden T-shirt, pantaloons and flip-flops in December, carrying a pink 'Jasper-Portus' guitar around the mall to drum up business. He played his signature lick, some flamenco run that he always played when demonstrating one of his guitars, and sang, "Come, hear the sounds of the future today, see your new guitar in MusicForYou, the little shop that explodes in your ears." Worst day of business the shop had all year.

Larry has encountered many characters while teaching guitar in England, the police officer who only wanted to learn Johnny Cash songs, insisting on it, then accusing Larry of not expanding his repertoire. A woman psychologist who spent her lessons dumping all of her own problems on Larry, then quitting because she didn't think she was learning enough guitar. A chap who lost his temper violently when he couldn't play something correctly and another chap who offered repeatedly and insistently to replace all the windows in Larry's house (which had blown units) for free (his business) and quit because Larry finally relented and said yes. Do not test the lord thy student.

The prize for this category goes to Fred, a grocery clerk who wanted to learn the electric guitar. Larry had to reinvent how to teach Fred because he had fingers like thick sausages. The thing is, Larry really liked this guy. Salt-of-the-earth and all that. But he had absolutely no aptitude for music. None. And he had no time to practice. Larry said it was the longest hour of his life. Normally, Larry would have said to such a student not to waste his money and perhaps take up some other hobby, but Fred loved his lessons. He didn't mind going over the same chord each week and Larry wracking his brains trying to figure out how to arrange Fred's fingers on the fret board for some kind of recognisable sound. But Fred had an unbelievable knowledge of bands, their personnel, their discography and what concerts they had played. He'd been to most of them all over Europe and had met many of the band members personally. He was a walking band encyclopedia. He loved talking about it to Larry and the two spent most of the time discussing bands, listening to Larry's CDs and Fred recounting some encounter with this or that rock star. That was all fine until Fred came to his last lesson looking very sheepish. He nearly cried. He said his Mrs. had told him he was rubbish and had no talent and she wasn't going to let him piss his money away any longer. She needed it for other, more constructive purposes. Poor Fred. Larry stays in touch. Fred is still working on his 'G' chord.

Larry learned a lot about character when he was back in Canada for his six month stretch. Mostly at a high school reunion he attended. Nothing is more revealing than meeting up with people decades after being with them as adolescents. Some have changed enormously, mentally as well as physically. Others never left high school. Some make it big. The rest of us wallow in a kind of self-imposed mediocrity. Still others fall on fortune and fame by luck. Many miss it by a hair. Larry just floats through life hoping to get lucky. His day is yet to come. He'd name names (after changing them) but quite a few of them will probably read this and Larry wants to be able to go to the next reunion without getting tarred and feathered. Still, who's he to judge? His life has had its share of good and bad moments like all his old colleagues, even the really successful ones. Sure there were characters in high school. Most of them still are, especially the fellow Village Idiot he met up with at an old friend's funeral just before Larry returned to LondonE. Paths still cross. Some fall off. Others never get back on track. Some have died. Larry told me he decided to leave all of them off the list. Sentimental fool.

He could write a book (actually he has) about the congregants he has shared space with over his years of being a preacher. Almost too many characters to list in this short work. Church people, in a word, are crazy....most of them anyway. Many of them demand without giving, criticise with impunity and generally moan about their miserable lives. There's always a crisis and everyone's problem is the most important in the world that the clergy are expected to solve. The preacher is the sole congregant not allowed to be a character. He or she (if the denomination in question allows women to be members of the clergy) must have a sterling character, be above reproach and be available 24/7. It's a miracle that Larry lasted 16 years on the job. And it certainly wasn't for the money. Refer to the chapter on Religion for more information about church types.

The last characters Larry had the good pleasure of dealing with in Canada lived in his mum's seniors building. She has her own two bedroom apartment and though certifiably blind, does pretty well on her own. She, like so many seniors, relishes her independence. And what an independent group lives in that one building. If becoming more stubborn is a sign of aging, the proof is in this building. Head-strong ladies and curmudgeonly men. Larry met them all. Mostly LondonOians. Most of the patrons are women. One woman in particular took it upon herself to run the place, or kept trying. Only because the administrator of the complex is a tough nut does there remain any equilibrium in running the show. The senior in question loves gathering the sheep to do her bidding, bitching about the menu (main meal at noon every day), the colour they painted the dining room, all that sort of thing. Larry's mum stays out of all that. Thankfully.

The alpha male of the complex is Ralph, a musician who had a stroke and has pretty well given up on life. Except for being a thorough curmudgeon. Older women are bitches. Elderly men are curmudgeons. Ralph sits in his wheel chair outside the front of the building staring at the ground most of the time. He likes Larry because of the music connection. And both are fans of The Toronto Blue Jays American league baseball team, although Ralph gripes about them too. He doesn't say much most of the time, but when he does be prepared for some verbal abuse, personal or otherwise. If you say white, Ralph says black. You say it's a beautiful day, Ralph will tell you it may rain or it's too hot or too cold. On a good day, he'll say, "Not bad." But that's also a very Canadian expression relating to everything.

Larry's mum has a soft streak in her. She likes to reach out to those who seem troubled. Some of that comes from being a minister's wife for so long. Mostly it's a natural tendency in her. Quite a few of the residents either don't have family living close by or any family they do have can't be bothered visiting them. Sad but true. Larry's mum tries to be a friend of sorts. She has two pet projects in the male population of her building. One is Charlie, an Englishman in a wheelchair who says very little but loves to sing the old English pub tunes. Knows all the words. Mum always joins in when Charlie gets going. When he does speak, he mumbles, so the others tend to ignore or shun him. Sad really.

The second project is Ralph, the more difficult of the two for sure. One day Larry's mum decided to do something nice for Ralph. She knew he liked a bottle of beer from time to time and Ralph was complaining about the hot weather as Larry's mum left the building to do a little shopping, pushing along her Cadillac of walkers (zimmer frame) and moving at a snail's pace, but determined to carry out the task. She stopped off at the Beer Store and picked up a six-pack, all for Ralph. Larry's mum slowly made her way back to where Ralph was still sitting, muttering to himself about the weather or something.

She said, "Ralph, I know you like beer, so I stopped at the Beer Store. I'm not sure what brand you like, but I got you a new beer my son really likes." She proceeded to hand the six-pack to Ralph.

Without even looking at it, Ralph shot back, "No thanks. Probably tastes like piss. Most new beer does. Drink it yourself or throw it away. I don't care." Larry's mum was nonplussed but fought back her anger. She hasn't quite given up on Ralph yet, but she won't be offering him anything else any time soon. Can you blame her?

The other thing Larry knows about characters? He's one. We've established that. I could tell you stories, but like I said, it would take a book. One important tidbit, though, buy him a six-pack of beer, any beer, and he'll never refuse it. He'll be your friend for life.

CHAPTER 14

SPORTS (MORE CULTURE)

'Get in there Turner, and for christ's sake hit something this
time.' (Larry's Canadian football coach in a game against Westview
Collegiate 1969)

Football is not football is not football. It's all rather confusing really. Real football is played in England. They use their feet. Canadian football is played with a ball, but the only time feet are used is when kicking on 3rd down, for a field goal or a kickoff. Only one player (maybe two) out of the whole team is responsible for this. Mostly, the ball is carried or thrown. Runball or Throwball would have been more accurate choices. Brits refer to it as American Football. Whatever you call it, Larry misses his beloved Toronto Argonauts who play in the Canadian Football League. He supports Arsenal Football Club in the English Premier League, a LondonE based club. Larry is not a fanatic for good reason. He loves sports, but gets too involved sometimes and his blood pressure rises. His kids used to tell him off for yelling at the TV screen when players did stupid things (in his estimation). "They can't hear you dad," they'd say. Larry told them he yelled loudly so they would hear him.

He's just as glad he lives in England now. No hockey (ice) team to yell at. No baseball team to upset him. No American football to rile him. You can have basketball. Never got into that much, but he does support the Toronto Raptors.

On that score he can't help himself. Anything Toronto is under Larry's careful scrutiny and concern. He can't say the same about LondonO. He does follow the London Knights hockey team. The Knights are part of the Ontario Hockey League (with a couple of teams from the US), a couple of tiers below the big league, the National Hockey League (NHL). One of his English cousins came over one Christmas while Larry was visiting his mum. They went to a Knights' game at the Budweiser Centre (Labatt's at the time….beer and sports eh?) and both have been fans since. He tried to go to a game at the university one year to see the Western Mustangs (of the University of Western Ontario in LondonO) play a football (not soccer) game against the visiting York University Lions team from Toronto (one of Larry's Alma Maters). It was sold out. Larry has seen no other sport in that fair city since.

I hope I haven't lost you yet. This chapter appears a little bit technical and not everyone is a sports fan, especially in these days of ridiculous salaries, spoiled players, greedy franchises and high ticket prices, game fixing and all kinds of other corruption. Larry thinks the whole scene is due to implode one day soon, but he still follows his teams from near and far, just not as closely as at one time. Money gets in the way of everything worthwhile. It usually ends up ruining a good thing to be sure. Playing any sport for the pure pleasure is a rare thing in the professional arena. You can still see it on local fields and in local ice arenas.

I apologise to North Americans reading this that I have to use the word ice when referring to hockey. Canadians just assume that hockey is played on ice. Not so in England. Field hockey is the game played there. Some ice hockey does exist and there are leagues which are usually made up mostly of expat Canadians and Americans. Some Brits play. Even American Football is gaining fans in England. Every year now the National Football League (NFL) sends over some teams to play regular season games at Wembley Stadium in LondonE. Always sold out as soon as tickets become available. Always way too expensive anyway. Implosion imminent. Back to basics would be the best approach.

Like playing on local fields. Larry sees football matches all the time around the part of southeast London where he lives. He hasn't yet stopped to watch, but he sees them playing as he passes. Young children football matches, adolescent and even adult matches go on every weekend during the season. Every spare piece of ground, even in Larry's beloved Danson Park, is turned into football pitches. Are these competitive matches? Certainly seems so. But no one is being paid, except maybe the referees, and the skills seem to be pretty good at every level. Playing for the pure joy of it. We have mostly forgotten.

The problem with professional sports and, for that matter, any organised sport begins with parents. On both sides of the Atlantic, parents create problems at games (matches) where their children are playing. Larry has seen it in the hockey arenas and on the soccer fields of Canada and on the football pitches in England. Vociferous parents verbally (and sometimes physically) abuse players from another team and even sometimes their own, referees, coaches and each other in the watching areas. Mums (Moms) can be as abusive as dads. Coaches encourage violence from their players and players can be abusive in their own rights. Wherever there is competition, there is the risk, a great risk, of violence occurring. Normal, you say. Therein lies the problem. Competitiveness is part of the human psyche. It will end up destroying us. Larry has felt it. He hates losing. Anyone who says they don't is either way too enlightened or not of this planet. Larry thinks they avoid competition for the same reason he does. He hates to lose. Poor soul. He's done his share of it.....losing that is. When we distance ourselves from anything, the thing appears trivial and even silly. Sports particularly. But we keep going back for more.

You might think the refined game of Cricket is above all that. Not much of it in Canada, played by Canadians anyway. It isn't a pioneer's sport like Lacrosse, which is actually a very violent First Nations game. Larry never played that. He was never coordinated enough. Cricket was the first love of his dad, in the area of sports that is. He played it in England as a youth and a young man. Larry's dad tried to follow the game as much as he could while exiled in Canada. He often disappeared on Sunday afternoons after church to some Cricket club pitch around Yonge Street and Wilson Avenue in Toronto. He insisted on going alone. No hanky-panky going on, just the pure joy of being by himself revelling in the sport he loved.

Larry remembers when his whole family visited England in 1978, sitting in his Nan's front room in Deptford watching a Cricket match with his dad and his brother. The others in the house thought they were having a nap due to the lack of sound coming from the room. They said they dared not enter for fear of waking the men. That's Cricket on TV for you. Little commentary and not a lot of action. A bit like watching paint dry. Fascinating game though. Larry's uncle (his dad's only brother) is also a fan. They played a lot of cricket together. Larry's uncle's (the uncle living in Canada) son (Larry's cousin), all 6'6" of him, plays in Canada, or did. He has all the gear. Larry's brother dabbled for a while too. Tough to make a real go of it in Canada. Canadians like action and fights and speed. They ought to give fast bowling cricketers a look. Hockey anyone?

The quote at the top of the page is from a coach Larry both feared and revered. Larry is a timid sportsman at best. Doesn't like broken bones or lacerations, that kind of thing. But he tries. Sort of. He has actually played more sports since his mid-forties than at any other time in his life, but retired at the grand old age of 53. It means for 10 years of his life, Larry played more sports at an age when most are so injured from their past sporting ventures, they have long since retired. Larry saves the best for the last. In one small village where he lived in Ontario he was playing hockey (not field) three nights a week in the winter, baseball and golf all summer and coached kids' soccer (football) and played as well. Best shape of his life.

But his old football (American…..actually Canadian) coach scared him away from competitive sports for decades after a season of injury and humiliation that could have left Larry scarred for life. Take that, coach, it's in black and white now. As Larry grows older, he knows full well that it wasn't the coach's fault, not all of it for sure. Larry has two crippling tendencies. He's a little uncoordinated and his attention span is very limited. Not a good combination in the sports arena. His golf game is erratic, his hockey slap shot is taken from the wrong anchor leg and he has a hard time keeping his eye on the ball in baseball or any sport.

Larry's football (we've already established which kind) coach wanted Larry to tackle more. One tackle during a practice ruined Larry's career forever…..not that he would have had one in the sport. So, Larry went out onto the field and made the tackle of his life, one still remembered by certain members of the old team. His then girlfriend's old boyfriend played for the opposing team. He was their quarterback, the star of the team. On one play, he carried the ball, charging to the outside of the pitch. Larry's side. Larry lowered his head, went low and hit the other guy with such force that he flew backwards, losing ground. The best and only tackle he ever made. Larry says he thinks he saw a tear of joy in the coach's eye.

His dad said Larry might have made a good bowler in Cricket. They were in Deptford Park during one of the visits back to the old country. Larry was 28 years old. His dad was showing him and his brother how to bowl and bat. One of those days to remember. In honour of his dad, Larry attended matches at the two Cricket shrines in LondonE his dad talked about, The Oval and Lord's. At Lord's, near the road crossing made famous by Larry's favourite Beatle album, England played Sri Lanka in a Test Match. He went with his dad's brother from Canada. Larry's dad would have loved it. At the Oval, the County of Kent played Surrey, Larry's dad's old team. Larry's brother was over from Canada to see that one. Memories.

The only time Larry attempted to play an organised sport in England, but never did, was with a cousin of his. Larry's cousin is a Rugby fanatic. At the time, the cousin played every Sunday afternoon at a pitch near his home for a team of guys that had been together for years. On this particular Sunday, the team was going to be a man short. Larry's cousin invited him to join the team for the game. Never having played rugby, watched it or being really interested in it, Larry had understandable trepidation. His cousin went over the basic rules and told Larry to stay on the back line and if the ball came to him to either get rid of it laterally (to one of his own players) or kick it down field (as far as he could). Simple enough.

Larry possessed no rugby gear and had only flimsy running shoes (trainers), a pair of cut-off jean shorts and a T-shirt. The day arrived. Larry stood on the sideline watching the carnage. He thinks the other lads on his cousin's team took one look at him and preferred playing a man short. A half an hour into the game, one of the players on his cousin's team had to be carried off the field on a stretcher with a suspected broken leg. One of the other players helping with the stretcher had blood streaming from under his headband down the side of his face. Larry's cousin asked if he'd like to come on for a while. Larry politely refused, saying he had a twinge in his knee from doing warmups on the sideline. Best decision he's ever made.

Larry's golf game was discussed elsewhere in the book. He never improved substantially from that day he began. He's had a few triumphs, but nothing consistent. He may par one or two holes in a round (of 9 holes, not 18) but double par the rest, sometimes even worse. To the point where he stops counting. He played quite often in Ontario, never in LondonO and never in LondonE or anywhere overseas. While back in Canada for half the year in 2013, Larry played a round at his old golf course where the owner, Jack Gorman, had given him a lifetime free membership when Larry left the village years before (the same golf course where Larry had started his golf career). It was good to see Jack and Rita again. Good people. Salt-of-the-earth types. Larry was staying a few days with old friends in the village and he and Steve Ferguson decided to go for it. Larry hadn't golfed since leaving Canada 8 years earlier. They approached the first hole. Just as Larry was about to swing, he heard a familiar voice shouting in his head, "Stick to tennis Rev.!" He should have.

And he does. This past summer, Larry and his best friend in England have gone to the tennis courts at Danson Park and bash the ball around for fun and exercise. The courts are full around the time of Wimbledon. Everyone is a pro then. Larry and his mate bought tennis racquets and decided to give it a go. They don't play games, just lob and chase the ball all over the court. No yelling, except at themselves and no competition (well, maybe a little). They go early in the morning to avoid everyone and play for an hour. Very amiable. No fights. No one wins. No one loses. The best way to play any sport. Challenging yourself.

Larry follows sport back in Canada on the internet. Can't help himself. And every Sunday he tunes in on his laptop to 740am on the dial, coming from Toronto, Ontario listening to two of his old schoolmates, Naz and Wally, discuss all the sports Larry continues to love from a distance. He is nothing if not sentimental, and a lover of nostalgia. He finds it's getting worse as he gets older. But you'll no longer find him on the pitch.

CHAPTER 15

HOLIDAYS

"No holidays, no country." Toba Beta, Master of Stupidity

One thing Larry knows absolutely, undeniably and unequivocally for sure. There are never enough holidays in a year. Especially true of LondonE and all of the UK for all that. Unless you go to school. Students always seem to be out of school there (here). And, as if the little beggars don't get enough time off, parents will often take their kids out of school during term to take advantage of cheaper holidays abroad. So much so that schools now fine parents for the inconvenience. Larry thinks school is a waste of time anyway, so he's ambivalent. That is until the kids are off and running around the streets screaming and clogging the trains and museums. Then he's all for public education, every day, all year.

But the rest of the hoi polloi get precious few breaks unless you happen to work for a very generous firm (business). In England, three civic holidays are marked on the Calendar, two in May and one at the end of August. They are known as Bank Holidays, but everyone gets them off and gets paid. The other five days are around Christmas and Easter. All other holidays are the stuff of negotiations between employer and employee. Canadian civic holidays are a little more generous, depending on the Province of residence and the mood of some employers. In LondonO, there are Family Day in February, Victoria Day in May (not even the Brits celebrate that Queen's birthday), 1st July Canada Day (celebrating Confederation in 1867), 1st August (Civic), Labour Day (beginning of September) Thanksgiving Monday (October) and the other usual suspects around Christmas and Easter. Kind of makes the Brits look stingy.

The French are another story all together, strange as usual and vaguely incongruous. They have eleven public holidays, but only May 1st is a paid holiday. The rest are all negotiable for getting off, but not getting paid. The strange fact is in the number of religious holidays for a nation that has all but given up on God. Ask any French person. Admitting religious belief, especially any Christian affiliation, is tantamount to announcing that you are a dolt or at least 'complètement fou/dingue'. The one for Mary going to heaven on 15th August is a riot. Larry still celebrates that just for spite. He can be testy that way.

The French don't really celebrate. Everything is quite underplayed and understated. Fireworks light up the sky on Bastille Day. Larry remembers being in Grenoble one summer and watching a sight and sound display raining down from La Bastille (the other one), the fortified mountain with a cable car ride to the top and a great view overlooking Grenoble. The music was Tchaikovsky's War of 1812 overture, a strange choice on French soil, but with real canon fire. The fireworks and the music combined are the best Larry has ever seen and heard. But other than that, there was very little else around the town to denote any celebration of the day France was declared a Republic. There were a few more of the Tricolor around, but that's it. Even Christmas is downplayed. The big holiday for France is the entire month of August. That's when the country all but shuts down and when Les Parigots (what people in the south of France call Parisians) invade the south and take up all the camp sites and generally treat the indigenous population as their lesser and not so sophisticated cousins who are there to wait on them.

The English are still a rather reserved lot. Larry blames the class system there. It still overshadows everything British. The only celebrations he has witnessed either have to do with England playing football and the Queen's Diamond Jubilee. The surprise celebration was during and just after the summer Olympics of 2012 held in LondonE. Before the Olympics, most Londoners shunned the coming event. It was too costly (mostly for Londoners), organisers were making a mess of Greenwich Park (site of the Equestrian events), the roads would be clogged because of the Cycle road races, the ticket distribution was a joke, the security measures were questioned because the company hired to provide them admitted they weren't ready.

The site came from reclaimed and appropriated lands in East London, the worst part of the city. Even the opening ceremonies were ridiculed as a portrayal of Hicksville Britain before anyone had seen them. But when the games began and everything was going swimmingly (mostly....there was a bit of a scandal with the tickets for swimming events), LondonE was one big party. Admittedly, the businesses in the centre of LondonE suffered. They complained that the promised extra traffic from all the tourists never happened. But this complaint got swallowed up in the general euphoria of the moment.

Other than those times, the English are rather subdued. None of the regular holidays elicit the need to let loose. Bank Holidays are a time to catch your breath before heading to the train or tube stations to work again or head to the pubs if you're on the dole (unemployment cheques/checks). The biggest annual celebration is a kind of oddity. Guy Fawkes night (Remember, Remember the 5th of November) celebrates the near blowing up of the Parliament buildings in 1605. Well, they call it Bonfire night when they are supposed to burn an effigy of Mr. Fawkes, but most people now wish he had succeeded and Guy Fawkes has become a kind of anti-establishment hero. The movie 'V' has done a lot to solidify this sentiment.

Still, the celebrations are wild on the 5th of November and for a week or so leading up to and after the date. The sky over LondonE becomes a sea of noise and colour. The air has the distinct smell of cordite for days, but especially on the night of the 5th (or any day either side when it doesn't rain). The first time Larry the Pyrotechnic (not Pyromaniac) Nut witnessed this he was utterly and completely mesmerised. The night of the 5th November, 2006 was one to remember. All around and over Larry's house the sizzles and booms of rockets burst gloriously and noisily. It must have been like the LondonE Blitz of the Second World War only in technicolour and much safer.

These were no backyard fizzle and pop firecrackers, the only legal ones that Canadians are allowed to buy. These are the big boys of the Fireworks world, still legal in the UK. Names like the 100 shot 'Awaken' at only £100 (roughly $180), 'Heavy Metal', 'Atomic Tornado', 'Bunker Buster', the 100 shot 'Dancing

Dragon' or the 72 shot 'Earth Shaker' at £150 ($275.50 Canadian) give you a lot of bang for your buck/pound. Single rockets are cheaper at around £15 ($27.55 Canadian) and quite a bargain for what you get. Can you imagine these going off in every garden (backyard) in the neighbourhood? Madness. There are some who detest the whole ritual which, it must be said, is repeated to a slightly lesser extent on New Year's Eve. Dogs and other pets particularly are prone to wince and hide at the sound of all the rockets going off.

Larry loves it. He says he hates to admit it, but thanks to the Chinese, celebrations are much livelier with fireworks. A better use for gunpowder to be sure. He usually goes to the big Bonfire Night display in Danson Park near his home. He can't get enough. In Canada he has to go to a public display to see the big berthas set off. Even then, it's nothing like Bonfire Night or New Year's Eve in LondonE and you have to travel some distance very often to see a great display, even if you live in Toronto and especially if you live in LondonO. Not so in LondonE. They are everywhere and more often. The best times to see fireworks in Canada is on July 1st, Canada Day, celebrating Canada becoming a nation in 1867. But Canadians are the first to make cutbacks in tough economic times and so one of the first things to go is the fireworks display. Larry searched high and low for a fireworks display in LondonO on Canada Day 2013. Nothing. From his window on the 5th floor of his mum's building, he could see a few of those backyard fizzlers. Not much of a celebration. In Britain they say, "Hang the bad times, let 'em rip".

Speaking of Canada Day, Larry was most surprised and delighted to discover that it was celebrated every year on the 1st of July in Trafalgar Square in the middle of LondonE. Canadians took over the whole Square for the entire day with a main stage, a ball hockey rink (no ice), booths advertising Canadian universities and showing off other cultural proclivities and food and drink stalls selling Canadian delicacies. Larry told me you could even get a Tim Horton's (known affectionately as Timmy's to Canadians) coffee and donut for only £10 ($18 Canadian). Highway robbery, but it's only once a year. Other goodies included Beaver Tails, Molson Canadian beer and bison burgers. And he says not to forget poutine (fries covered in melted cheese and gravy).

The lineup for Timmy's was always the longest, but not to worry. Larry met all kinds of expats from all over Canada waiting for their fix. One year he wore his Toronto Maple Leafs hockey jersey to the affair and was roundly applauded by most who are true Leafs fans and soundly booed by those wearing Montreal Canadiens (Les Habs) jerseys….all in good fun. One year, two guys on stilts, one wearing the TML jersey, the other a Habs jersey, clunked around the Square good naturedly bashing each other with foam hockey sticks. Ah, those crazy Canucks.

The entertainment was first class, Blue Rodeo, Jann Arden, The Tragically Hip, lots of big Canadian names and many lesser with equal talent. First Nations dancers, traditional down east music (the Atlantic Maritime Provinces) and even a rapper or two graced the main stage all day long. Larry would have given them a tune or two but was never invited. He had offered. They don't know what they were missing let me tell you and I ought to know. No bias here.

This year, 2014, Larry went on the Canada Day/Trafalgar Square website for information about the event and to see who would be there. Horrors. It had been cancelled. And so had the similar event in New York and Hong Kong, sponsored by some corporations. They claimed that the economic climate did not allow them to carry on with the event. Larry despises corporations at the best of times, so you know this news did nothing to change his mind. They are all about profit, not people, he says. The Canadian government (aka Prime Minister Stephen Harper, whom Larry says can try to sue him for that remark, but good luck getting blood from a stone) was asked to step in and keep it going after 8 years of celebrations, but expats are expendable and so that plan was kyboshed. An alternative event was to be held at some castle, but it had an admission price and was too far away. Celebrating Canada can wait.

Folk on both sides of the pond (Atlantic Ocean) take holidays. Brits like to go to warmer climes, even in the summertime. Campaigns have been launched to keep Brits at home spending their money in Britain. It works to some extent, but the sun and warmth of Spain, Tenerife, Cyprus, Majorca and even Florida calls. Brits like to camp, but campsites are nothing like they are in Ontario, unless you compare it to the KOA (Kamps Of America, also in Canada) campgrounds. Larry has tried camping in England, once at a farm/campground in Kent and the other in Cornwall on the edge of a cliff. Neither experience was what he was used to in Canada. Camping in Ontario is the best in the world according to Larry. But he is slightly biased. Just slightly.

Larry's family camped all around Ontario when he was growing up. He still remembers the smells and sounds of those summers, the sounds of crickets and bullfrogs, people talking around their campfires late into the night, the warmth and comfort of the sleeping bag on an air mattress and those camp meals cooked on a propane or naphtha gas powered stove, the night lanterns, digging rain trenches around the family size tent and watching fireflies turn their lights on and off in the dark. Then graduating to a tent trailer, the more posh way to camp, travelling all the way to the east coast of Canada in 1967. Larry loved the camping trips that were situated near water. Swimming was fun and riding the waves into shore on Lake Huron was as memorable for Larry as it would be later for his children. They met some good folk (campers are the salt-of-the-earth types) and learned about the natural world, not always the easy way (see Flora and Fauna).

One time, when Larry and a high school mate took another friend on his first canoe trip in Algonquin Park, Ontario, the unexpected happened. They were on Burnt Island Lake and found a good camping spot. They hauled their food out of the canoe in a gunny sack and tied it to a branch up in a tree after their meal. Larry stood by the cooking fire, cleaning up. The newbie camper went to the edge of a clearing to relieve himself. There was no sense of panic in what came next. The newbie said, "Hey fellas, there's a bear coming this way." Larry and his school mate both said, "Yeah, George (his real name), sure." He repeated, very calmly, "No, really fellas, there's a bear coming this way. Honest." A moment later in lumbered a large black bear, heading straight for Larry. His school friend Doug (his real name....the guy Larry couldn't get to in Collingwood) ran down to the water's edge, ready to jump in the lake to swim for it. He yelled back to George to drop and play dead. George obeyed.

The bear came towards Larry who had no time to move. All he had on was a pair of cut-off jean shorts and some hiking boots. Larry stood rigidly still. The bear approached him from the rear, raising itself onto its hind legs, sniffing Larry from ankles to neck. 'I'm dead' Larry thought. Suddenly, the bear raised its nose in the air, sniffing at something. It dropped to all fours and headed over to an open chocolate powder container (Nestle's Quick for those who remember the stuff). The lads had brought it to mix with the nearly unpalatable powdered milk. The hairy beast grabbed the container in his jaws and ran off, past the prostrate George and across the clearing. Gone. Larry breathed again. He was glad he hadn't soiled himself. The young men were just gathering to talk about the experience when another bear entered the scene. All three lads headed down to the edge of the lake, but the bear stopped and sniffed the air. Larry learned a valuable lesson that day.

"Don't worry guys," Larry calmly announced, "Our food is safe. Bears don't climb trees."

"I think they can," Doug retorted.

And it did. Straight up the trunk and out along the branch. Somehow it reached one of its paws into the gunny sack and of all things plucked out the only bag of cookies (biscuits) the lads had brought with them (French Vanilla Creams….a black bear's choice). That was the last straw. Larry and the other two grabbed the paddles out of the canoe and charged toward the tree, yelling and screaming like madmen. The bear dropped from the tree and ran off. The guys loaded the canoe and headed for an island in the middle of the lake. There they found some other refugees who had encountered some bears. Mucho story telling around the campfire that night. Not much sleep. Bears, it seems, can also swim.

On another holiday canoe trip into Algonquin years later with two of his children, Larry lived through a tornado with trees crashing around the tent in a violent storm that seems to be becoming more a part of southern Ontario weather. Larry had to wait until the next day to hear about the damage the tornado did to the park. Camping in England is a doddle compared to that, despite the rain. Larry hasn't even mentioned the black flies and the horse flies that take chunks of flesh when they bite, let alone the clouds of mosquitoes that are the vampires of Canada. A few are around in England, but nothing the same.

The most dangerous part of camping in England is usually the gangs of youths who decide to camp right beside you, make their mess and their noise and generally disrupting everyone's peace around them. Give Larry bears any day. The English prefer trailer camping, mostly fixed trailers in trailer parks where there are amusements and programs for the kids. Tent camping is mostly for other Europeans who visit Britain or when the English attend music festivals like Glastonbury. One of Larry's guitar students attended the last one with fifty other people, all in tents. British camping. Camping in France remains a mystery to Larry. He's never tried it there. He doesn't think he'd like it anyway.

One name keeps coming up when the English talk about holidays. It would appear that most of them at one time or another went on a holiday to a camp known as Butlin's. The story goes that a man named Billy Butlin (and later his son Bobby Butlin….you can't make this stuff up) began and then ran some summer programs around the UK to provide affordable holidays for average people. The accommodations were known as chalets lines, basic accommodation. Over the years these have been upgraded to include en-suite bathrooms, the original sites having had only communal ablution areas.

Many of the sites were sold in the 1980s and 90s because of fierce competition from foreign companies (what else) but the name remains on three key sites around Britain. Larry talked to people who had been to one of the camps at one time or another, some going back year after year because it was affordable for families. All sorts of attractions, programs for kids and entertainment were available to make the time spent fun for the family. Many future British music stars and comedians got their start at these camps. The other two major Holiday Camps and Parks are Pontins and Haven, the latter being the more popular these days. Both have been down-sized over the years and run pretty well the same kind of establishment as Butlins. Larry says it all sounds dreadful. But then his children are grown up.

In Ontario, summer camps are a place to send the kids for a week or more to give the parents a break. They can also be a great way to take in the great outdoors and learn a few skills. The parents of camp kids may have gone to a summer camp as well at some point in their lives and they send their own children out of some nostalgic memory of friends made and good times had. When Larry went through his religious phase, he spent a number of summers as a chaplain to one particular camp run by a different church denomination to his own. He was gradually phasing out of the belief structure in which he'd been raised (see Religion) and was focusing on teaching Astronomy (not Astrology) to the campers. He also led the camp in singing all the camp songs. His chaplain times at camp are still remembered as fun, not preachy. The way it ought to be for children. All three of Larry's children attended the camp over the years. The youngest went all the way to Assistant Director. These camps have canoe lessons, archery, rock-wall climbing, high ropes lessons, campfires with skits and songs, craft sessions, hikes, overnight camping trips, the lot. All in the good old outdoors. That camp has meant a lot to Larry. It grounded him. And he needed it.

In all three countries, but especially in Canada and England, drinking alcohol is the primary objective of most holidays. In Ontario, the civic holiday to commemorate Queen Victoria's birthday is known as the May 2/4 weekend, not signifying the date on which the holiday is held (which is the actual case), but the number of bottles in a case of beer, 24. According to some reliable statistics that Larry gives no credence to, Canadians drink more beer per capita than any other nation in the world. Canadians like to kick back and guzzle beer, have BBQs and watch sports. Sounds vaguely American, but I'm not writing about them. Larry remembers those weekends. Most of his were of the wholesome variety being a preacher's kid and all. While others were out getting shit-faced, Larry would be at a church BBQ or at some public event with fireworks, paltry compared to those around Britain. But we've already been there. Only in later years, when Larry no longer cared about the taboos (he blames his English cousins for corrupting him), did he imbibe with the rest, at someone's cottage or in their backyard (garden).

The English drink pretty well all of the time, with some occasionally going on binges. They don't need holidays for an excuse. Alcohol is available everywhere, from supermarkets to the corner stores. There are pubs everywhere, though because of the tough economic times and cheap supermarket drink many pubs are closing all over LondonE and elsewhere in the UK. But people still drink. Lots. On holidays the drinking escalates. Sometimes, when the youth of Britain are on holiday in farther climes such as Greece or some part of Spain, they get into all sorts of alcohol related trouble. And not only the youth. Those who ought to know better, the so-called grownups, can be found causing trouble in local bars abroad even when there is no football match to be found. Some British men have a certain aggressive swagger that defies logic when it comes to being sensible in sensitive situations. Larry avoids such circumstances to the best of his ability. He's a lover, not a fighter. Even a number of British women are not averse to the arena of violence if things don't go their way. Larry says British women have a sharp edge to them. Best stay clear when they are in a snit.

A kind of self-perceived entitlement follows some English people when they travel abroad. They are never as English as they are when in another country. It is as if the Empire still lives within them and all about ought to recognise the fact. Larry thinks they get loud and obnoxious because they are oblivious to anything going on around them. They only think about being English during the World Cup of Football (soccer) and then only when England may have a chance to win it. 2014 was not one of those years. But the English do like to travel. Australia and New Zealand have become destinations of choice, not only to holiday but to live. They speak English there and the food is quite similar. The English love Canada with all its space and ruggedness and have a love/hate relationship with the United States.

When Larry first visited England, 17 years after his family left there, he stayed at his nan's in Deptford, SE8 (southeast). Before he returned to Canada, he went down the street to a shop that sold sporting goods….an old shop where everything in it looked time worn and dust laden. He wanted to get his dad a Millwall Football sports bag. Millwall being the local team, it seemed only proper to get their gear for his dad. Larry entered the shop asking the rather elderly lady behind the counter if she had such a bag. She looked at him and announced quite haughtily that she did not. Larry persisted, sensing something was amiss. He told the woman that his mum and dad had lived around there and Larry wanted to bring back a token of his dad's past. The woman's eyes raised slightly. She asked who that might be. Larry told her his mum's name and suddenly the old crone's face lit up.

"You're Doll's (Larry's mum's mum) grandson? Well, that changes things. I think I might have one or two Millwall bags left. I'll just go put the kettle on for a cup of tea. I want to hear all the family news."

It was a pleasant hour or so he spent there after that. The lady apologised for her earlier behaviour. "I thought you were a Yank, you see, and we still don't like them around here because of what they did to our women during the war." Basically, American service men on leave in London (not all of them to be sure) had flings with local girls, then dumped them afterward. Some of the girls had babies and some had cheated on their husbands who were fighting the war abroad. Not a good scene. She added that the Canadian soldiers were much more civil and many of them married their girls and took them back to Canada or stayed on in England. That was her version of things at any rate. Larry ended up leaving with a free Millwall bag. When he gave it to his dad and told him the story, his dad said thanks, but he was an Arsenal fan. Oh well, at least it didn't cost him a farthing.

Americans love to holiday in England. The sense of history here is palpable. For many it's like going back to their roots, the Motherland so to speak. Even though they fought to gain independence from Britain and won it 1776, the fascination is still there. Canadians visit because of the history and the link with the Monarchy. Many still have family here. But there is another quality, already mentioned elsewhere. This land of England is magical. Larry thinks so. I think there's something to it, but have yet to be convinced. Larry tells us to look at the records. Stonchenge, Avebury, Thornborough and Mayburgh henges all line up in these ley lines that tap into the energy of the planet. More than one person has said this to Larry and he has tried to explain it to me. For those who take the Chakras seriously, there are maps about showing us where the earth chakras lie. It's all about energy and attraction. Everybody following this? Well, keep going, there is a point Larry wants to make.

Two of the earth chakras are located in England, the 4th chakra, the heart, is located around Glastonbury and Shaftesbury. Glastonbury is said to be the Avalon of the King Arthur tales and where Joseph of Arimathea (Jesus's step-dad) was said to have brought the Holy Grail (yeah, right). Every June they hold the biggest music festival in England. Can you feel the energy? Just ask any responsible and serious dowser how powerful the whole of the south of England feels. Those rods go crazy in so many places. And no wonder. The 6th chakra, the 3rd Eye, is a floating chakra, but at the moment is also located around Glastonbury. So that makes two chakras right here in jolly old England. Weird stuff, but believed by many in this Age of Pisces, a religious age that gets more fanatical towards the end (the Age of Aquarius being some 150 years from now). The ley lines from all parts of England run through a hub, LondonE. Larry asks if there's any doubt the hordes are attracted to this city given its abundance of pure energy attracting them. He says you can feel it in every part of the city. Especially Soho.

No one has the needed time to see everything LondonE has to offer or soak up all the energy the city emits. Larry can't say the same for LondonO which has a weak ley line well to the south and where no chakras even come close to it. Like he says, in the middle of nowhere with nothing around it. They ought to have left it as fertile farm land from the beginning. The energy is low Larry says. You can feel it (or you can't). To be fair, it really is like comparing those 1976 Honda Civics to one of the new 2015 Type R Civic models. Larry's brother had one of the early versions (came in yellow). He called it Barney. Good name for a rust bucket that went to rubble. In this analogy, LondonO is the old model, though the newest city and LondonE is the Type R. There is no comparison except they are both called Hondas. The only true comparison might be with southeast LondonE. Not too much magic going on there, not yet anyway. Larry says he's working on it.

It means for the moment that as many people come to the Borough of Bexley (southeast LondonE) to holiday as they do to LondonO. Larry has no statistics, but it seems to him that when he goes into London proper, there are a lot more people about not from LondonE than are found visiting the Borough of Bexley. Yes, there is Hall Place in the borough, built around 1540 by the Lord Mayor of London as his country house. Henry VIII stayed there a few times. The Red House, designed, owned and lived in by William Morris the designer in the 19th century has a tea room and gift shop. The 12th Century ruins of Lesnes Abbey in the well-kept Abbey Wood is relatively close to a train station (but in a dodgy part of the borough). Danson Park is a treat for locals with its lake, annual fairs, gardens, manor house, lawn bowling and tennis courts. Hardly the stuff to attract millions of holidaying tourists. Still, there is more historical attraction in every part of the Borough of Bexley than anywhere in LondonO.

That's not to say LondonO is without its attractions. Some of them are quite interesting. TripAdvisor rates 53 attractions worth a look. Number one on the list is Boler Mountain, a big hill really, but has skiing and tubing in the winter and mountain biking in the summer. Larry has never seen it. Number two is a theatre, Aeolian Hall, the third is the Budweiser Centre (formerly known as the

Labatt's Center and still called that by most locals) where ice hockey games are played and world class talent comes to sing, tell jokes and generally entertain. In the centre of the city is Victoria Park, number five on the list and beside it St. Paul's Cathedral. It had to be. It's a London after all. This cathedral, though, was built between 1844 and 1846 on the ruins of an earlier church built in 1843 and burned down in 1844. St Paul's in LondonE was built on the site of a church from 604AD, the latest version designed by Christopher Wren (the architect, scientist, preacher, etc.) in the late 1600s. No comparison.

Back to LondonO with Eldon House, the oldest surviving house built in 1834 (attraction number eight) and a rather lovely Pioneer Village with 33 original and replica structures and tens of thousands of artifacts from the 19th century. But most people go to Black Creek Pioneer Village in Toronto or the magnificent Upper Canada Village in Morristown, Ontario near Kingston (another university town but with far more character in a much more scenic location). Near LondonO, located in a Conservation area closer to the village of Mount Brydges, is the First Nations village of Ska-Nah-Doht (a village stands again), the replica of a thousand year old Iroquoian village by a river. Larry has no information about this place as he has never been, but it sounds like a great day out if you like driving. There again, people usually go to the Huron/Ouendat Village and Huronia Museum north of Toronto with a more scenic drive enroute as well. Larry has never been there either but hears it's the best. He was supposed to go one year with his high school class. But he did something foolish (he begged me not to say what) and wasn't allowed to go. And so he never did.

The 2013 World Figure Skating Championships were held in LondonO. No one, except maybe LondonOers knows why. Many of the competitors complained that there was very little to do there. Coaches probably loved it because of fewer distractions. One Eastern European competitor was heard to say how excited she was when she heard the competition was in London. She was making a list of all the things she wanted to see and do. She was so disappointed when she discovered she would be going to LondonO and not LondonE. In LondonO's defence, it must be pointed out that the ice would have definitely been better.

But the clincher for Larry was a story in a LondonO newspaper about his Blues guitar hero Joe Bonamassa (an American) who played the Budweiser Centre while Larry was there in May of 2013. According to Joe, he was more afraid walking the streets of downtown LondonO in the middle of the afternoon than he had been the day before in Detroit, Michigan. He says he was accosted by an 8-year-old boy who tried to mug him. The number of people asking for handouts and badgering him for booze had clearly affected Larry's guitar hero. The reporter was embarrassed and went on to say his town was becoming a place where no one wanted to live. And it seems the same goes for holidaying there. Larry hastens to add that people have been mugged in LondonE too, but that's not the point. Joe has played in LondonE a number of times and has never uttered a disparaging word about the place.

Holiday where you will. Larry prefers the beaches of Majorca, though he wants to see more of Britain, especially the Lake District. He says he would like to visit Scotland again before they gain their independence, but he sees that as unlikely. As I write this, the Scots have just voted against independence, except for Glasgow, a few of the other major urban areas and Andy Murray, the tennis player (and his mum). Glasgow would become a separate country if it were allowed. Might happen yet. Scots still hate the English. They ought to hate the politicians and leave the rest of us be. Larry seems to think it's really all about money. No more handouts if they had left. Always the money, the oil and the past. But, Larry shall still visit there some day. Despite Glaswegians, the country is a beauty. Pitlochry awaits.

CHAPTER 16

TELEVISON: AND OTHER SILLY TECHNOLOGIES

"The game's afoot." (Larry's son just before playing 'Call of Duty')

Larry is addicted to television. He hates to admit it. And no, he doesn't just watch the documentary channels. At the moment he has one of those SmartTV boxes, a computer that runs the TV, or something like that. Don't ask Larry the Luddite. Anyway, he has Netflix and somehow got signed up to Amazon Prime. Now he has access to all those old TV series he hasn't seen, whole seasons of Jack Bauer and '24'. He loves ScFi, so he's locked into all kinds of those series. Lots of movies to choose from too. He tried really hard to get rid of TV when he got back from Canada in the Fall (Autumn) of 2013, but it just keeps showing up, pleading with Larry to take it back. He's an old softy and gives in every time.

He was sick of the cable services he had. They cost less than they do in Canada. Don't get Larry started about Rogers and Bell, the two companies that dominate (actually monopolise) the Ontario media landscape. It really is a scandal….unless you are a member of the Rogers family and own stock in Ma Bell. What Larry's mum pays a month for her TV and phone (no internet) is not just a scandal, it's a con. Crooked. So sue me. In Britain there are the big three, British Telecom (BT, around forever and stale as buggery), BSkyB, the bully of the bunch and Virgin Media, Richard Branson's baby that promises much and delivers less. There are a lot of smaller companies vying for my TV, telephone and internet quid (£), giving consumers much more choice than in Ontario and some of them are extremely reasonably priced. Competition in the market place is good for the consumer. Obviously, Canadian companies couldn't care less about them. Profit rules in Ontario.

When Larry was back in LondonO with his mum for those 6 months in 2013, he needed the internet. He had to call the folks at Rogers to get it hooked up. The cost was nearly prohibitive. Well, no, it actually was prohibitive. His mum had to help with the cost. The price per month for the internet alone was 5 times more than what Larry paid for internet, TV and his phone line for 3 months in LondonE. Add in Larry's mum's TV and phone and you get the picture. Still, it's all a con. What the salespeople tell you and what is delivered are two different things. And the damned thing kept going wrong. Not only the internet, but the TV too. The Rogers guys kept coming and trying this and that. In the end they said it was a problem with the initial set up for the whole building. Radical changes needed to be made. The bills might be higher. Another con.

Back in England, Larry was having all kinds of trouble with his Virgin Media. He had switched from Sky because they used a dish fixed to Larry's chimney that was never put on right and quit every time the wind blew and the rain poured down. Which was a lot. The guys they sent to fix things were a bit like Laurel and Hardy except they were not funny, not in a humorous way anyhow. They tried to change the dish in the dark and got it wrong, dropped a ladder on Larry's friend's car and didn't own up to it and generally messed about. Virgin promises better quality because they use fibre-optic cable, nothing above ground, so the weather can't affect it. Troubles galore ensued. Repair guys were sent out and each one kept attaching these little boxes to the cables saying they would boost the signal. It wasn't until the last guy came that the truth came out. This guy was diamond. He and Larry got talking about hockey (the real hockey....ice hockey) because he played with a bunch of Canadians. A bond formed. He told Larry that his house was the furthest from the relay box so Larry's signal was the weakest. The fibre-optic cable only ran to the box and from there plain old conventional cable was used to the house connection. Larry would always have problems. He quit them too.

Larry blames his addiction to TV on his parents. His family had a TV right up to the time Larry was a teenager then decided to get rid of it. No Mork and Mindy for Larry. The mid 1960s to the late 1970s are a mystery to him television-wise, a quasi-religious, anti-technology phase Larry's parents went through. Some would say it was a bold thing to do in an age of burgeoning technology, some might say 'Bravo. Wish we could do it and read more and have more meaningful family times'. But they didn't and neither did Larry. Any TV he saw was at a friend's. But he always felt guilty. After a time, he actually got used to it. But the day he got back into watching it, he was hooked forever.

Coming back to England presents some problems for television viewing for Larry. He grew up with some memories of British TV, like Sooty the puppet and Bill and Ben the Flowerpot men, but those were as old as the hills. He missed out on a lot of programs, so the stars of British TV were now a mystery to him. When an old television personality retires or dies or changes venues, everyone knows who it is and has countless stories about them. Larry has no idea who they are talking about. The same goes for radio DJs and other celebrities from any number of media. Larry knows the big guns, but there are so many minor ones. He knew so many back in Canada. He had to learn about new music groups, the ones that never made it to North America. When he left Canada, none of this was familiar when he arrived in England. He couldn't talk about the TV personalities he knew back in Canada, the newscasters, the comedians, the writers and musicians. No one has heard of Peter Mansbridge in England. Media is a regional and a territorial thing.

Before you all break into floods of sympathetic tears for our poor Larry, be assured that the newness and freshness of British TV has its advantages too. Larry was reintroduced to Dr. Who, Only Fools and Horses and met (virtually of course) a host of television personalities he would otherwise never have known existed. Like starting over. Fresh. Trouble is, most TV these days is rubbish. All those channels and so very little going on. Even the interesting channels like the History Channel and Discovery repeat things over and over. Their budgets don't allow for continuous new and exciting programming. What is left is a host of reality shows that really aren't all that real and become tedious very quickly. Most follow a shallow premise and are more gossip oriented than entertaining.

In Britain, those TV programs come in the form of regional young people acting like idiots to gain attention. Made in Chelsea (LondonE), The Only Way is Essex (don't get Larry started) and Geordie Shore (Newcastle types). They claim to be reality based, but they quickly become silly soap operas. Then we have the talent show and the find a new singing star show, the ballroom dancing show plus the selection of has-been celebrities thrown together in an Australian jungle to see who wins a popularity contest while eating kangaroo penises.

When Larry was with his mum for six months, her TV was confined to Murder She Wrote, Third Rock from the Sun and old British sitcom reruns on, of all places, the God channel. Larry supposes Canadians think God loves British TV programs. Maybe not The Inbetweeners, it's crude. But then who knows? Larry thinks British original programming like Downton Abbey and the new Sherlock Holmes are far better written than any Canadian equivalents. That may be a bit unfair seeing that Larry hasn't been exposed to a lot of Canadian content in the past 9 years. But you definitely see more British TV in Canada than the other way around. Even the very popular Ice Road Truckers, filmed mainly on Canadian roads in Manitoba and the Yukon, is an American production. Larry says he saw a program advertised about searching for the next Canadian female model, but please.

Larry watched some TV in France. Not much. He was otherwise occupied, viewing it only for instructional purposes. He remembers the strangest thing he saw was John Wayne speaking French….dubbed of course. Watching French TV was a chore. Any comedy was short lived. The French are a serious lot who love to kill off their heroes and end things badly. Their version of reality TV. He has no idea what's on these days. He supposes John Wayne still shows up from time to time spouting his tough talk in French. Can't do anything about that walk though.

Larry pays for a TV license in England. The British Broadcasting Corporation demands it. A tax on TV really. It means if you have a tele, you pay the tax. Even if you never watch anything on the half dozen BBC channels, you have to pay the license fee. The BBC claims it makes great programming, but it has been getting more scarce over the years. Too top heavy and the twits they put in charge run it further into the ground. The internet has had a hand in that too. The Canadian equivalent is the Canadian Broadcasting Corporation, presently being run into the ground by the present Prime Minister of Canada. If it goes private, regional television will suffer. Imagine, no Innuit programming. Oh my. The real death knell for the CBC came when it lost its contract to broadcast Hockey Night in Canada every Saturday. Guess who won that battle? Rogers….the monopoly folk. Larry has his suspicions.

When Larry returned to England in 1973 there were three channels, BBC 1 and 2 and ITV (Thames television for LondonE). Not a lot of choice, but then with hundreds of channels you could say the same thing. Very little is new. The best television comes from America under the name of HBO and Showcase, two programmers that reshape the boundaries for television. Breaking Bad is a great example of that. Larry loved it. Gritty, savvy, emotive, the works. It explored the whole human psyche. We are a scary lot. Still, no one does time pieces like the Brits. So they still have that. Downton Abbey is the proof. Canadians and Americans love it. Old England isn't finished yet, even though Grytpype-Thynne might have something to say about that.

Larry has little time for all the other technologies. He never plays those video games. Call of Duty and Grand Theft Auto mystify him. He has no co-ordination for them anyway. Larry's son plays. When Larry visits him, he tries to get his dad to game with him. Larry flatly refuses every time. He watches his son's fingers roll all over the game paddle, pushing this and pressing that with a speed that defies the laws of physics. Larry did try it once with his son. It was a Hockey game, the NHL. Larry thought he at least understood the game, so why not. After about a minute, it was 23-0 for his son. Larry retired permanently from gaming. He understands the allure, just not the time it takes to get into it and the levels to be achieved. It goes on and on. Ask anyone with children addicted to gaming.

Larry's addiction to TV doesn't seem so sinister after that. They are all time wasters really. But nothing comes close to the Smart Phones for letting time get away. Larry had what they call a brick for years until December 2013 when he became eligible for a new phone from the company with which he deals. He was perfectly happy with his Pay-As-You-Go brick until those near and dear to him coaxed him into joining the 21st Century and getting the Smart Phone (Mobiles in Britain, Cells in Canada). He ended up with the Samsung Galaxy Ace 3, just arrived, the new rival to the iPhone5 and cheaper with a contract of two years. But who can keep up? He had it a month and some new model came out, same as the iPhone. There was the i4, then the i4c, followed by the i4s, then the i5, i5c, i5s and soon the i6. Either technology is changing nearly daily or the purveyors of scam are very good at bamboozling us. Larry thinks it's the latter. That's probably because he's old and his addled brain refuses to accept such rapid change and the need to keep up with it. He'll never figure out how to use all the Apps (Applications). His kids try to tell him. Even his up-to-date brother has tried. To no avail. Larry stares at them blankly when they try to explain how to use this or that feature. Took him a month to figure out how to answer an incoming call. He was tapping away at the little green phone on the screen when his best friend said, "I think you have to slide it. See the arrow? It's moving to indicate where to slide it so you can take the call." Larry said, "Oh." Good thing he doesn't get many calls.

Larry says he doesn't want an iPad. He has a laptop. He has no idea how to use it except for very rudimentary tasks. He has to keep asking his best friend to get him out of trouble. Thankfully, one of his guitar students is an Information Technologist (IT) for a huge European company and has helped Larry out of several jams. For a long time Larry thought the IT of a company was actually, well, you know, 'It'....the boss or the go-to person. He has a lot to learn. But he won't. He'll revel in his Luddite mode, sneering at those who have embraced technology willingly and successfully. He needs no gadgets to prove he is an intelligent man. He even said he wanted to go out and buy one of those old-fashioned type writers with clacking keys, a ribbon and a carriage that goes ding. Don't expect another book for a while, unless his best friend persuades him otherwise. Could happen. Don't hold your breath.

CHAPTER 17

MUSIC

'If music be the food of love, play on.' William Shakespeare (perhaps) 'Twelfth Night'

I save Larry's favourite topic till the last. Music. One thing Larry knows about music (and it's considerable) is that we need much, much more of it in our lives, like humour. All kinds of music too. Larry's favourite music is the Blues, in all its forms, from Robert Johnson to Joe Bonamassa, but especially BB King and Eric Clapton. He has an enormous collection of CDs. He once had lots of vinyl, but went through a crazy conservative Christian streak back in the late 1970s when he threw away all his secular albums and only listened to Christian Rock. That phase lasted until the mid 1990s and died completely in 2004. He never went back to vinyl….wishes he had, but he's stubborn that way….and now has a great collection partly due to his teaching the guitar and keyboard to people who have eclectic music tastes, everything from Johnny Cash to Metallica.

Larry owes his love of the Blues to his dad who played Lightnin' Hopkins, Sonny Terry and Brownie McGhee and other old greats when Larry was but a young lad. He thanks the British for bringing the Blues back from near extinction when white Americans had given up on them as mainstream music. You can blame that maniacal penchant for detesting or being afraid of anything Black back in the day. Between that and revulsion toward Communism that went beyond rational and you can see why the Brits, stuffy as most of them were, had to bring some semblance of sensibility to the table. The musical table in this case. Thanks to the likes of Long John Baldry (who later emigrated to Canada), Alexis Korner, John Mayall, Eric Clapton, The Rolling Stones and other Rock music groups of the day, the Blues were kept alive and eventually even caught on in North America.

Larry followed the Blues scene in Canada during the 1960s and 1970s, before he became a manic Christian, thanks also to his dad, a hard-line preacher of the Gospel, as we noted earlier. Whiskey Howl, McKenna/Mendelson Mainline, The Downchild Blues Band and others were the stuff of Larry's early love for electric Blues. But it was folk music that got him started. He played in a group that sang the songs of Peter, Paul and Mary, Joan Baez and Bob Dylan. His music heroes were Gordon Lightfoot, Bruce Cockburn, Joni Mitchell and Ian and Sylvia, all Canadians who played folk/rock. But the Blues were always first in his heart. He wouldn't properly learn how to play them until he was in his 50s.

Meanwhile in England, music was becoming a many splendoured thing. Larry remembers his visit in 1973 as a musical smorgasbord, everything from Perry Como (who had two in the top 100 that year in Britain), Al Martino and Shirley Bassey to the Beatles and a chap named Gilbert O'Sullivan. A novelty song called 'Winchester Cathedral' came from the land of Larry in 1966. Where does time go? Larry's favourite was by a chap named Mungo Jerry with his hit 'In the Summertime' from 1970, still getting airplay in 1973 and beyond (mainly in the summertime when the weather is hot). Then there was Tiny Tim, the ukulele player/singer. Though an American (they have had their musical idiosyncrasies too), he even did a concert in The Royal Albert Hall in LondonE, usually reserved for the big guns of music. The music from the British Isles is eclectic to say the least. Musical tastes in Britain change as quickly as they change their briefs (nickers). A look at the top 100 hits over the decades from the 1960s reveals this. In 1966, Jim Reeves and Frank Sinatra were No. 1 and No 2 on the British charts while 'Good Vibrations' by the Beach Boys was only No. 12 and the Beatles' 'Day Tripper' was No 13. Even the limp 'Yellow Submarine' by the Beatles beat them at No. 3. In 1967, the numbers 1, 2 and 5 spots were held by Engelbert Humperdinck. Procul Harem's 'Whiter Shade of Pale was only No. 4, a far superior song. In 1968, Louis Armstrong's 'What a Wonderful World' came in at No. 1 ahead of the Beatles' 'Hey Jude'. Unbelievable.

In 1969, when everyone ought to have known better, the Archies 'Sugar Sugar' was No. 1 ahead of some of the greatest Rock music ever written. Even Frank Sinatra was getting into the Top 10 with 'My Way' (No. 9). 1970 saw Rolf Harris in the No. 5 spot with 'Two Little Boys'. Let's not go there. In 1971, Benny Hill made it to No. 15 with 'Ernie: The Fastest Milkman in the West'…. talk about novelty songs making it big. The rest of the 1970s fared no better….'72 'Mouldy Old Dough' by Lieutenant Pigeon No 5, '73 Perry Como No.9 and No. 22 (poor Stevie Wonder's great song 'You are the Sunshine of my Life was only No. 100), '78 'The Smurf Song, by Father Abraham and the Smurfs No 7. The 1980s are forgettable unless you really liked all that electronic nonsense. Worth mentioning just for the sake of it is 'Zoom' by Fat Larry's Band, No. 29. Nothing much improved in the 1990s. Lots of great music came out, but in 1999 on the Eve of a new Millennium, Britney Spears was No. 1 with 'Baby One More Time'. When Larry arrived in 2006, the No.1 hit was Shakira's 'Hips Don't Lie' featuring Wyclef Jean (whoever that may be). Not to be outdone, 2014's No. 1 to date is Pharrell Williams' 'Happy'. The better version is Weird Al Yankovic's parody of that song 'Tacky'. It's all bad, but not bad in the good way.

Much of the music scene in Britain at the moment is a soulless thing. Musical pap is the order of the day. Larry blames it on Simon Cowell, but it's bigger than that. Shallowness lies deep in the hearts of people who are brainwashed into accepting and following, like sheep, any trend they are told to like and buy. This is true of more than just music, but Larry says this particular medium more than any other is of the soul. It needs to be fed with honesty and integrity. So the emotions have to be real, not contrived, and physical movement has to come from deep within the soul, not from some drunken stupor. Pure music is not for profit. You can earn a living from it, but off it is another thing entirely. Music is borderless. It is at the core of all that it means to be human, lifting us beyond the mundane. That's why when there's talk about dropping music programs from schools (always the first thing to go….as are any of the arts) a little more of the soul is lost. That's why when many serious musicians are treated like an afterthought, an injustice is committed.

Larry met an English woman at a Keb' Mo' concert at Union Chapel in LondonE not long ago. Keb' Mo' (Kevin Moore) is an American Blues singer/ songwriter who sings and plays more than just the Blues. He is well known in Canada and the United States as well as the rest of Europe, but not in England. If they don't know you there, they don't go to hear you. Union Chapel is a nice enough venue, but it ain't The Royal Albert or the O2 where a performer of Keb' Mo's stature ought to be playing. That's Larry's opinion at any rate. But he's not alone. The English woman, who works in musical circles in Britain, confirmed Larry's suspicions. She said the English don't treat visiting musicians very well (low pay and general disdain), especially if they are not known….not known because club music and pop rule the day in Britain, rap too for many strange reasons….and so many great artists bypass LondonE and the rest of Britain. They want to go there, but why would they?

Another characteristic of British bands and other musical acts is the way the media treats them when they do have a modicum of success. The word would be abysmally, tearing down anyone who becomes successful. It's probably why there are a lot of good bands out there that are little known or struggling and mostly self-effacing. This is the only country Larry knows where the celebrities apologise if they feel like they've been overexposed. Larry says the Brits love to champion an underdog but tear him or her apart if the underdog ever makes it big. It is a phenomenon without precedent, especially among the male population. Probably why most of the males Larry knows in London always greet him with a put-down or a biting remark first. If you take it seriously or personally, you're in for a world of trouble. Best to either counter it with something witty or leave the country. In North America, the opposite is true. They champion success and ignore the underdog.

Larry says that music in Canada is quite well-balanced and well represented from all sectors of the business. He dislikes calling music a business (Larry wanted me to say hates, but I said that was a bit heavy). But let's be real. That doesn't mean musicians are treated any better in Canada. It's a Canadian tradition that to be a real star you have to go to the land to the south. Many of Larry's musician friends have had to make it in America. Larry says he'd name them, but you can Google them anytime. Most of them eventually return to Canada either because they crave a more subdued, sane way of living or they are sent packing from America. You know who I mean. Canada has been a haven for other musicians and artists from around the world who want to detox, hide out, chill out or just hang out.

When Larry was in his transitional stage from a man-of-the-cloth to a musician-and-a-sloth, he conducted a nighttime wedding in one of those beautiful Ontario Provincial Parks. After the ceremony, he was introduced to an Englishman (friend of the bride and groom) who happened to have been the original bass player in a little English band known as The Kinks. Larry had formed a band from church and community members that got together every so often to put on Coffee Houses in the village in which he then lived. They played cover tunes from all the old bands, nothing religious, unless you call music a religion.

Peter from the Kinks said to Larry, "I hear you have a combo going. Need a bass player?" Naturally, he said it in a LondonE accent. Larry's group already had a bass player, not altogether reliable, but even so, what an opportunity. Peter reclaimed his old Rickenbacker bass from a mate in California and sat in with The Rockin' Reverend, as Larry was known, and his band of reprobates. One day Larry asked Peter what the heck he was doing in this backwoods (almost literally) part of Ontario. "Taxes," says Peter. "Avoiding them." Larry asked no more questions. Sadly, Peter left this world a few years ago due to kidney failure. The Guardian newspaper in LondonE wrote an obituary for Peter on 27th June, 2010. One paragraph read, "In 1980 (actually, it was the 1990s, but we'll forgive them) Peter moved to Belleville in Ontario, where he played with a local amateur church band." Larry smiled.

One of Larry's Canadian folk heroes is Gordon Lightfoot who is 76 years old as this is being written. They met once at a house party Larry attended with someone who knew someone who was there. Larry has played Lightfoot's music since, but never as big as when he was a missionary in France in the 1980s, working at a radio station that broadcast Christian messages into North Africa and the Middle East. Larry played the guitar for the station staff get-togethers (all religious music back then). He worked in a different department to the broadcast area, the non-glam area. One day the head of broadcasting asked Larry if he would come on air and play something Canadian for the folks of North Africa and the Middle East. Larry didn't hesitate. It had to be Lightfoot and it had to be distinctly Canadian. He sang two pieces, 'Canadian Railroad Trilogy' and 'Christian Island'. The response was overwhelming. Even though Larry had credited the songs to Lightfoot, many listeners wanted to know who this Canadian singer, Larry Lightfoot was and would he please tour their country and where could they buy his music. All those great songs Larry wishes he had written. There was a call for an encore but Larry had moved on by then. He went back to Canada to become a preacher, the pastor of disaster.

While in France in the 1980s, Larry noticed that music was becoming electronic, an almost soulless sound. Everywhere. The Thompson Twins, Boy George, Tears for Fears, The Pet Shop Boys, Talking Heads, even the likes of Peter Gabriel, Eric Clapton and all the Jacksons got on board what Larry calls the musical sleaze wagon that was the 1980s. There never was a shallower time. Lots of money around, new drugs being marketed (not the strictly medicinal kind), new technologies like CDs (Compact Discs, not Cross Dressers), VCRs (Video Cassette Recorders) and advanced PCs (Personal Computers, not Political Correctness). All to entertain and inform, in an advertising way. Larry may have been in the missionary mode back then, but he started back on the road of listening to secular music. Most of it was from the French market and not that great; France Gall, Jean-Jaques Goldman (who is actually very good), Johnny Hallyday, Téléphone and an assortment of other groups and chanteurs and chanteuses, all on the charts in France. Larry was missing his Blues.

Strange thing is, Paris is a hotbed for Jazz and Blues. But the 1980s belonged to the soulless ones. All the good music had to wait until the new Millennium to make a comeback. That's not to say there was no good music at all in the 1980s, it just wasn't getting radio time, which is probably true of most years. But for radio in France during those years the lightweight tunes rose to the top. People want the easy. Then there are those who don't listen to music at all, the dullards. No interest in anything except a plate of food in front of them and some kind of sporting event on the tele. You find them in any culture. Larry has no time for them.

Some holdover music groups from the 1970s prevailed. Larry saw Supertramp in Paris in 1982 and again in Avignon in 1986 (without Roger Hodgson). Some good new groups were on the scene as well, REM, Bruce Hornsby and so on.

But Larry was between his Christian phase and the new busting out persona, not allowing him at the time to explore the wider music field. Besides, he was still in France and the pickings were slim. He started catching up when he left the Mission and returned to Canada. The 1990s was a good decade to rekindle the musical fires. The blaze came in the new Millennium. Larry never looked back after 2004.

He determined that he shall have music wherever he goes. Since moving to LondonE, Larry has attended many concerts, the most in his life. Clapton (twice), Jeff Beck, Mark Knopfler, Fleetwood Mac (without Christine McVie unfortunately), The Eagles (unfortunately without Don Felder), James Taylor, Neil Young, Bob Dylan, Fleet Foxes, Kings of Leon, The Dave Matthews Band (best concert ever) and more. He also has gone to hear some great Blues artists including Buddy Guy, Joe Bonamassa, Keb' Mo', Kenny Wayne Shepherd, Derek Trucks, Robert Cray, Seasick Steve, the Canadian Layla Zoe and then some. Larry says his old ears can't take much more. He may be retiring from the live circuit.

But you can see him around town, earphones on (low volume….he's going deaf with all the years of ear abuse), listening to good tunes, especially while travelling on the trains going into and back from LondonE. He took a pilgrimage on train and tube to Abbey Road studios (outside the gate like everyone else) and had a picture of him and his eldest daughter crossing the famous crosswalk as featured on the Beatles' Abbey Road album. Music is his new salvation he says. He loves it all and will continue to do so until he can no longer hear or move. Though musical tastes differ between the cultures, the lines are steadily becoming more blurred. Good old Rock 'N Roll brought down the Berlin Wall and eventually the Russian Soviet Empire. Something about music, especially Rock music, changes things. Maybe it's the vibrations.

Good vibrations. That's what it's all about. As with Shakespeare (and he had a lot of music in his plays….if they were his plays), let the world overdose on music. We need it now more than ever, all types of music. Larry didn't want to go way back into the history of music in his three countries and cultures. Needless to say the only indigenous music of Canada comes from its First Nations people. Larry was invited one summer to a Powwow by a Native Canadian friend of his. The music and dancing were inspiring. The same summer Larry went to a Celtic Festival near LondonO. Great music there too. It's everywhere in a variety of cultural settings. You just have to look. Festivals have sprung up all over the place (too many in Britain every year to keep track of) with all genres of music. Good for the soul, good for the planet.

Larry would like to busk in LondonE. He has built up a treasure chest full of great cover tunes. He has written some of his own, but he feels that there are so many great songs out there, why not give the folks what they want….some Beatles, a bit of Bob Dylan, lots of Blues, Springsteen, Neil Young and perhaps a few more up-to-date pieces like Passenger, Bon Iver and Oasis. You can't go wrong in LondonE with 'Wonderwall' says Larry. He has played a few places but needs to get out there and perform before his fingers seize up. Look for him if you visit the city. He'll probably try to find a spot along the River Thames on the south bank. Everyone has to have a dream.

EPILOGUE

"And as we walk in the dimming light, Oh darling, understand
that everything ends." Death Cab for Cutie

Thus it ends, this journey into the stuff that has made Expat Larry, well, Expat
Larry. Some of it makes him nostalgic. Other parts cause him to become re-
flective, journeying into his very soul to discover himself anew. Most of it elicits
laughter. Larry thinks life is funny. He might have been saying something in
a sermon and suddenly felt the urge to laugh at it. He would be conducting a
funeral and want to make faces and do silly dances. Seriousness continues to be
a problem for him. Mostly he laughs at himself. He needs to. But none of you
dare. His is a private dance between normalcy and madness with one taking the
lead over the other from time to time. That's probably why he sees things in a
slightly skewed way. Agree with him or not, he is entitled to his take on a mad
world. If you think your views are better, you write about them. Better still, don't
bother. This is going to be the last book written on the subject. The world needs
no more.

Larry had asked me to include a chapter on architecture. One of Larry's dear
friends is an architect in Canada and he wanted to show off by comparing buildings in LondonO to LondonE with types and structural lingo and all that. The
truth is Larry knows nothing about the subject. Gothic, Romanesque, Art Deco
and some others neither I nor Larry could be bothered researching. His friend
lived in LondonE for a year a number of years ago and probably knows more

about the buildings here (except maybe for the newest ones) than Larry will ever know. The only memorable one for Larry in LondonO is now a government building where Larry had to go to apply for his Canada Pension. It looks like something out of a Chicago gangster movie. In LondonE Larry says he wouldn't know where to begin but Tower Bridge remains his favourite. He doesn't like LondonE City Hall. Looks like a cake with its layers sliding off in the middle.

Larry loves where he lives now. But he may yet make a move to another endroit. You never know. He's not sure where he'd go. Like with LondonO, there are plenty of other places in England with a little more to them than the southeast of London. Other parts of Kent look nice. He has yet to visit the Lake District. He loves the walled city of York. Cornwall and Devon are beautiful, but flooding is an issue. He loves Canada, big and boring as it is. But he'd settle somewhere near the Rockies out west before going back to Ontario to live (unless someone gave him a cottage on a lake in Muskoka).

Larry could easily have stayed and lived forever in the south of France. The food, the weather, everything agreeable. Except the French. In the end he chose England. The food is still good and mostly fresh. Plenty of good beer and wines. He tolerates the English with their peculiar personalities and odd way of saying things. He feels more at home in Ontario, but never LondonO, which is where he'll probably end up. Sod's Law, as his best friend says.

For those who still haven't bothered translating the passage in the weather chapter, the weather report goes like this, Weather Forecast: 'Today the sun will shine, but there may be some windy days next week. In the morning there may be some rain (Frarney is short for France 'n' Spain....but who knew?) but no snow or the dreaded ice.' You are all much richer for it.

Larry says he'll remain on Twitter for the time being. His use of that social medium has waned since his beginning just over a year ago. He's prepared for the Twitter fallout and abuse from LondonOers. Probably have to change his name next time he visits. And visit he must. His mum, his daughter and his brother, along with assorted nieces and a nephew still live and work there.

You might have noticed the sentences and paragraphs got longer after the Preface and as the book progressed. This is none of Larry's doing. It is entirely my fault. Charles Dickens is one of my favourite writers. Old habits die hard.... or not at all. So, to get back on track for an instant, I leave you with this.

And so adieu to you all. Maybe sometime we'll meet, have a pint and reminisce. In the meantime, relax, be yourself, tell your stories, live.

Note: The former paragraph was 140 characters to the letter. This Twit is signing out.